The Reminiscences of

Rear Admiral John S. Coye, Jr.
U.S. Navy (Retired)

U.S. Naval Institute
Annapolis, Maryland
1983

Preface

The real joy in Admiral Coye's professional life was commanding ships, which he did exceptionally well. The most noteworthy part of this oral autobiography is his description of service as skipper of the submarine Silversides during World War II. He also tells well the story of the years prior to World War II in which his duty in the USS Shark and the USS R-18 well prepared him for command of his own boat. As a skipper he had the same frustrations as many others in making attacks on Japanese ships and then having his efforts foiled by faulty torpedoes. He managed to persevere and to sink many Japanese ships, both in solo operations and as a wolf pack member and wolf pack commander. In fact, he was so successful that he was put in charge of the prospective commanding officers' school at New London in 1945. After the war, he held a succession of submarine jobs, commanding a division, squadron, and the tender Fulton.

Interspersed with his submarine duties are descriptions of Admiral Coye's other assignments, including duty as a junior officer in the heavy cruiser Northampton and destroyer Monaghan, attendance at the Armed Forces Staff College and Naval War College, service on the staffs of Commander Operational Development Force doing ASW development work; Commander Second Fleet while planning exercise Strike Back; the strike warfare section in OpNav; and Commander in Chief Allied Forces Southern Europe during a staff consolidation. As a captain, he enjoyed the pleasure of commanding the heavy cruiser Rochester while she was Seventh Fleet flagship. As a flag officer he commanded the naval forces in the Marianas, Amphibious Group Three, and Training Command Atlantic Fleet in addition to the CinCSouth staff assignment.

This oral history is the joint product of a number of individuals: Commander Etta-Belle Kitchen, U.S. Navy(Retired), who conducted the interviews; Ms. Sarah Henderson, who prepared the index for the volume; and Mrs. Deborah Reid, who transcribed the tapes and prepared the smooth-typed version.

                                                     Paul Stillwell
                                                     Director of Oral History
                                                     U.S. Naval Institute
                                                     December 1983

REAR ADMIRAL JOHN STARR COYE, JR., UNITED STATES NAVY (RETIRED)

John Starr Coye, Jr., was born in Berkeley, California, on April 24, 1911, son of the late John S. and Mabel S. Coye. He attended high school in Wilmington, Delaware, and on June 14, 1929 entered the U.S. Naval Academy, Annapolis, Maryland. Commissioned Ensign upon graduation on June 1, 1933, he subsequently advanced in rank to Rear Admiral. His date of rank is July 1, 1961.

After graduation from the Naval Academy in June 1933, he was assigned to the USS Northampton, flagship of Cruiser Division 4, on the West Coast, and in March 1935 was detached to assist in fitting out the USS Monaghan, then being built at the Navy Yard, Boston, Massachusetts. From her commissioning on April 19, 1935, until December 1936, he served as Assistant Engineer of that destroyer which cruised to the British Isles, Peru, Alaska, and made a Presidential fishing cruise in 1936.

He was a student at the Submarine School, New London, Connecticut, from January to June 1937 and served as Engineer of the USS Shark from June 1937 until October 1940. He was next assigned to the USS R-18, which was recommissioned at the Philadelphia Navy Yard on January 8, 1941, and later served as Commanding Officer of that submarine from April 1942 until April 1943.

After a brief period of instruction at the Prospective Commanding Officers School, Submarine Base, New London, he reported in June 1943 to the Submarine Command of the South Pacific Force, for assignment as Commanding Officer of the USS Silversides. That submarine was awarded the Presidential Unit citation for outstanding performance in combat during her fourth, fifth, seventh and tenth war patrols, and he was personally awarded the Navy Cross and two Gold Stars in lieu of the second and third Navy Cross, the Bronze Star Medal, and the Legion of Merit, with Combat "V" authorized for the last two medals. Citations follow, in part:

Navy Cross: "For extraordinary heroism as Commanding Officer of the USS Silversides on war patrol in enemy Japanese-controlled waters...During two engagements with heavily escorted hostile convoys, (he) delivered accurate and devastating torpedo attacks against the enemy, sinking and damaging a number of Japanese vessels. Despite persistent counterattacks by the opposing forces, he skillfully evaded the enemy and brought his craft to port without material damage or casualties..."

Gold Star in lieu of the second Navy Cross: "For extraordinary heroism...in enemy Japanese-held waters on December 29, 1943, and on January 2, 1944. After contacting a heavily escorted enemy convoy, (he) fearlessly penetrated the formidable screen and launched a series of brilliantly executed attacks to sink or extensively damage more than 26,500 tons of hostile shipping. Skillfully evading the ensuing countermeasures, he cleared the vicinity to resume his aggressive patrol. Endangered by a Japanese submarine on January 2, (he), by his exceptional alertness, quick thinking and positive action, saved his gallant ship from a three-torpedo attack. His inspiring conduct and the outstanding performance of his courageous officers and men throughout this highly successful war patrol were in keeping with the highest traditions of the U.S. Naval Service."

Gold Star in lieu of third Navy Cross: "For extraordinary heroism...during the period from April 26, 1944 to June 11, 1944. Despite unusually strong enemy escorts, including active air opposition, he skillfully penetrated these escort screens while avoiding air attack, and through his daring and aggressive determination delivered torpedo attacks upon enemy ships. As a result of these well planned and brilliantly executed attacks, he successfully sank five enemy ships totaling 23,600 tons and damaged three additional ships totaling 18,000 tons..."

Legion of Merit: "For exceptionally meritorious conduct...as Commanding Officer of the USS Silversides during her eleventh war patrol against Japanese forces in the Formosa and Kyushu areas from September to November 1944...Commander Coye contributed materially to the success of his ship in sinking a 10,000 ton enemy tanker and in damaging two hostile escort vessels. Directing the formation of a protective screen around a friendly submarine which had been crippled by enemy action, he skillfully avoided injury to his own ship despite enemy counterattacks and succeeded in escorting the damaged submarine safely to post..."

Bronze Star Medal: "For heroic service as Commanding Officer of the USS Silversides, in action against enemy forces in the Pacific War Area during her ninth war patrol, from February 15 to April 8, 1944. Pursuing highly aggressive and daring tactics against the enemy,

Commander Coye launched a series of torpedo attacks which resulted in the sinking of two hostile ships totaling 7,500 tons and, skillfully evading all countermeasures after each attack, brought his ship back to port..."

Rear Admiral (then Commander) Coye was detached from Silversides in December 1944, after commanding her during six successful war patrols, during which he was credited with 14 confirmed sinkings. He returned to the Submarine School where he served as PCO Instructor for two years. He received a Letter of Commendation, with authorization to wear the Commendation Ribbon, from the Commander in Chief, U.S. Atlantic Fleet and was cited in part as follows: "For meritorious conduct while serving as the Senior Administration Instructor of the Command Class course of the Submarine School, U.S. Submarine Base, New London, Connecticut, from January 1945 to September 1945..." In March 1947 he became Operations officer on the Staff of Commander Submarine Squadron ONE, and from June 1948 to July 1949 served as Commander Submarine Division 52. He was a student at the Armed Forces Staff College during the next five months, and from January 1950 until February 1952 served on the staff of Commander Operational Development Force, at Norfolk, Virginia.

He next had command of the USS Fulton, a submarine tender, and when detached in September 1953 he assumed command of Submarine Squadron EIGHT. He was a student at the Naval War College during the winter of 1954-1955, then was assigned to the Staff of Commander SECOND Fleet/Commander STRIKING Fleet Atlantic as Operations Officer and later as Chief of Staff for Plans, Operations and Readiness. During this period he helped to plan and participated in the large scale NATO exercise STRIKE BACK.

In January 1958 he took command of the Rochester, which at the time was serving as the flagship of Commander SEVENTH Fleet in the Western Pacific. In January of 1959 he was detached from the Rochester for a tour of duty as Assistant Director, Strike Warfare Division, in the Office of the Deputy Chief of Naval Operations, (Fleet Operations and Readiness), Navy Department, Washington, D.C.

In September 1961, following his selection as a Rear Admiral, he became Commander Naval Forces, Marianas with additional duty as the Commander in Chief, Pacific Representative, Marianas-Bonin. In October 1962 he was ordered to duty as Commander Amphibious Group Three. He assumed commander of Amphibious Group Three on January 5, 1963, on board the Amphibious Command Ship USS Eldorado. As an Amphibious Task Force Commander, he conducted several large scale amphibious exercises. On April 30, 1964 he reported as Deputy Chief of Staff to the Commander in Chief, Allied Forces, Southern Europe and in February 1966 was ordered detached for duty as Commander Training Command, Atlantic Fleet.

This was a busy job, involving not only training ships at Guantanamo, supervision at various Fleet Training Commands, introduction of the Naval Tactical Data System and also special emphasis on fire fighting, particularly for the carriers.

He retired in Norfolk on August 1968. Upon retirement he was awarded the Legion of Merit (Gold Star in lieu of Second Award). Citation follows, in part:

"For exceptionally meritorious service from August 1966 to July 1968 while serving as Commander Training Command, United States Atlantic Fleet. Exercising outstanding leadership, planning and managerial abilities, Rear Admiral Coye contributed significantly to the successful training of personnel, thereby ensuring the readiness of the fleet to support national policies. Through his timely implementation of effective training programs and his judicious utilization of available resources, he maintained an outstanding level of performance during a period of changing and challenging requirements generated by increasingly sophisticated ships, weapons systems, and electronic devices..."

In addition to the Navy Cross with two Gold Stars, the Legion of Merit with Gold Star and Combat "V," the Bronze Star Medal, also with Combat "V," the Commendation Ribbon, and the Ribbon for the Presidential Unit Citation to the USS Silversides, Rear Admiral Coye has the American Defense Service Medal, Fleet Clasp; the American Campaign Medal; Asiatic-Pacific Campaign Medal; the World War II Victory Medal; and the National Defense Service Medal.

He is married to the former Elizabeth Gabriel of Worcester, Massachusetts, and has three children: Beth Frances Coye, John S. Coye, III, and Sarah Louise Coye. Beth was also in the Navy, and retired as a commander in August 1980.

Rear Admiral Coye's official address is Coronado, California.

AUTHORIZATION

The undersigned, Rear Admiral John S. Coye, Jr., U. S. Navy (Retired) does hereby release and assign to the United States Naval Institute all his right, title, restrictions, and interest in two interviews between the undersigned and the Oral History Department of the United States Naval Institute, recorded on 15 and 16 September 1982 in collaboration with Commander Etta-Belle Kitchen, U. S. Navy (Retired). The tape recordings of the interviews shall be the sole property of the Naval Institute. The copyright in both the oral and transcribed versions of the interviews shall also be the sole property of the Naval Institute.

Signed and sealed this 20th day of December, 1983.

John S. Coye Jr.
Rear Admiral John S. Coye, Jr., USN (Ret.)

Interview Number 1 with Admiral John Starr Coye, Jr.,
U.S. Navy (Retired)

Place: Admiral Coye's residence in Coronado, California

Date: 15 September 1982

Subject: Biography

Interviewer: Commander Etta-Belle Kitchen, U.S. Navy (Retired)

Q: I appreciate your letting me come. I thank you and I am looking forward to doing the biography. Since we would like to have this as a complete biography, I think it might be nice for us to start at the beginning. So why don't you tell me a little bit about where you were born, your early days, and we'll begin with that.

Admiral Coye: I was born in Berkeley, California. My dad was a chemist. My mother had been a professional musician. I was born in 1911. I lived in Berkeley for maybe three or four years, and then my dad went back to Iowa State University in Ames, Iowa, to teach, and I moved there.

It turned out that my wife's dad was also a teacher there, and so the families were well acquainted, and it turns out we have a picture taken when I was about five and my wife was about four.

Q: Isn't that interesting!

Coye #1 - 2

Admiral Coye: I lived in Iowa until I was about nine years old, and then my dad had a job in New York City with General Chemical Company, and we moved to Long Island, and I lived there until I was about 13, I guess, my first year in high school. Then my dad took a job in Wilmington, Delaware, and we moved to Wilmington, and I went to Wilmington High School.

Q: It sounds as though it might have been with Du Pont, since he was a chemist.

Admiral Coye: No, he was with the General Chemical Company, which later changed its name to Allied Chemical and Dye, I believe.

After I graduated from high school, my dad, who had always loved California, wanted to come back to California. So we drove across country in 1928, and we lived in Berkeley again for a while. At this time, the Depression was starting and actually, I didn't really have enough money to go to college, so I worked as an apprentice machinist in Berkeley, and later my dad went down to the Mojave Desert, where he was chief chemist for the American Potash and Chemical Company. I worked there for a while as a machinist's helper.

I had early aspired to go to the Naval Academy. When I was in Wilmington, I went with the Hi-Y YMCA Club to a conference in Annapolis. There I had my first view of Annapolis, and I had applied, while I was at Wilmington High School, for an appointment to the Naval Academy, but at that time there were no vacancies. The senator had

Coye #1 - 3

said he was sorry, but he didn't have any vacancies. It turned out that the next year he did have a vacancy, and so he sent me a telegram. By this time I was in California and he said that he had a vacancy and asked if I still wanted the appointment. I said, "Of course," so that was how I got appointed to the Naval Academy by Senator Thomas F. Bayard.*

Q: Did you have any particular interests in high school that you think led you to go to the Academy--any particular sports or particular work that made you wish to go to the Academy?

Admiral Coye: Well, I had always been interested in the sea. We lived on the edge of the Delaware River, and I could see the ships going up and down the river all the time. I remember the Navy ships that went up there, some of the destroyers and whatnot that were going up to the Philadelphia Navy Yard. As a matter of fact, I can remember in high school writing what at that time the English department called a thesis. It really wasn't a thesis. I chose as my subject the history of submarines.

Q: Did you?

Admiral Coye: Yes, so I had an early interest in submarines.

---

*Democrat-Delaware.

Q: How did you get your information on which to write your thesis?

Admiral Coye: I got that out of reading books and things like that. Actually, I wasn't an athlete in high school. My dad had been captain of the football team at Iowa, but he felt that youngsters in high school weren't properly coached and could very easily get injuries that would ruin the rest of their lives. So he wouldn't let me go out for football in high school. But he himself had been a very good athlete, my dad had.

Also, as a youngster, I loved music, my mother having been a professional musician. I played and studied the clarinet and went to the Curtis Institute of Music up in Philadelphia and studied with the then-solo clarinetist in the Philadelphia Orchestra.

Q: Where were you living then?

Admiral Coye: In Wilmington.

Q: And went up from there up to Curtis Institute?

Admiral Coye: Yes.

Q: How long a period were you there at Curtis?

Admiral Coye: I used to go up there once a week.

Coye #1 - 5

Q: Oh, you went up a day's travel back and forth?

Admiral Coye: Right.

Q: Oh, I see. Of course, that's a very famous institution.

Admiral Coye: Yes. Later, when I got in the Navy, I found that playing the clarinet really wasn't compatible, because you had to play in an orchestra, and I was always busy off on ships or something like that, so I eventually gave that up.

Q: But as you speak to me, it seems you had a well-rounded series of interests before you ever went to the Academy.

Admiral Coye: Yes. Before the appointment to the Academy, I had done well in high school. I was a good student, and I had been president of the National Honor Society at high school. I had good recommendations to Senator Bayard, whom I had never met personally, but he appointed me and gave me a principal appointment, which was really unusual in those days, because the Depression was just starting to come on, and it was hard to get an appointment to the Academy. There were so many trying to get in to get the education, I feel that our class of 1933, which entered in 1929, probably had some of the best minds in the country in it at that time.

Coye #1 - 6

Q: I think it's particularly unusual, because you had gone to California; he must have thought you were very good material.

Admiral Coye: Yes. Of course, Senator Bayard had just been defeated for reelection, and I personally think he felt that some of his Delaware citizens had let him down.

Q: So he said, "I'll show you a thing or two." Well, all to your benefit, of course.

Admiral Coye: It's interesting how the roads of life come to the crossroads and one way you take and the other you don't, and how it works out.

Q: I know that. But I think it's interesting that you say that because of the Depression that there were such fine minds in that class.

Admiral Coye: Yes, I really think that's true.

Q: Do you want to name some of the outstanding or some of your friends that were...

Admiral Coye: Well, of course we had Tom Moorer there, and there are lots of them.* Our class had a higher percentage make flag rank than any other class. I think we had over 50 admirals and we only graduated 432. Do you want me to go into the rest of the class now?

Q: Well, I think Admiral Moorer is a prominent name. Are there others that were your good friends or whom you think you'd like to include in your biography?

Admiral Coye: There are so many of them, that I'd rather not.

Q: Sometimes there is a person who is, say, your best friend or is an outstanding person that comes to your mind immediately when you are recollecting.

Admiral Coye: Probably our closest friend is Admiral Schade who was ComSubLant.** He was also a submariner, and he's a very smart officer. There are numerous others.

Q: I'm sure, with 50 admirals, there would be a lot. Now, what were your main interests while you were at the Academy?

Admiral Coye: Of course, when I was at the Academy, we all took the

---

*Admiral Thomas H. Moorer, who eventually served as Chief of Naval Operations and Chairman of the Joint Chiefs of Staff.
**Vice Admiral Arnold F. Schade, USN(Ret.), who served as Commander Submarine Force, U.S. Atlantic Fleet, from 1966 to 1970.

Coye #1 - 8

same course. Now they have a choice of courses, but we only had a choice of what language we would take, whether French or Spanish.

I did well at the Academy in the engineering subjects, electrical engineering, steam engineering were my best subjects. My languages and English and whatnot were my lower subjects.

Q: Well, you had had some background in the engineering field.

Admiral Coye: In sports, I went out for the football team, but, as I mentioned earlier, I hadn't played in high school, so the kids who had played in high school did better, and they got on the team and I didn't.

Q: Did that break your heart?

Admiral Coye: It didn't break my heart. I later went out for the boxing team, which I didn't do very well in that. I was cannon fodder. We did have a good boxing team at the time. "Spike" Webb was there as the coach, and we were intercollegiate champions.*

Q: I remember his name.

Admiral Coye: Yes, but I was strictly a cannon fodder type.

---
*Hamilton M. Webb.

Coye #1 - 9

Q: Oh, that's too bad. Well, wasn't "Moon" Chapple on that?

Admiral Coye: Yes, Moon Chapple was there.* He was there my plebe year. Moon was a first classman and he, of course, was intercollegiate champion in boxing, as I remember.

Q: He was my first commanding officer.

Admiral Coye: Oh, was he?

Q: And he used to regale me with tales of "Spike" Webb and the people who were on that boxing team. Then you did become an ensign in what year?

Admiral Coye: I graduated in 1933. If you remember the Class of 1933, this was still in the Depression, and funds were short, so they only commissioned half the class. Do you remember that or heard about that?

Q: Yes, I had heard of it.

Admiral Coye: So, I fortunately was in the half that got a commission Later on, of course, most of the rest of the class came back in with

---

*Wreford G. Chapple, who served as a submarine skipper during World War II.

Coye #1 - 10

World War II coming on. They could see that they would need all these officers, so that in the subsequent year, in 1934, they commissioned most of the rest of of my class, and then some of the rest of them came in in 1935 and in 1936.

Q: But immediately, what happened to the half that was not commissioned? Did they leave the Navy?

Admiral Coye: Yes. They left the Navy. They gave them a year's pay as a midshipman, as I remember, and I think they put them in the Naval Reserve, but they went out and got civilian jobs.

Q: I had never actually heard that description of what happened. As you say, I had heard about half the class graduating, but it never occurred to me what happened to the poor fellows that didn't. And you say they came back in subsequent years.

Admiral Coye: Right.

Q: But they wouldn't have had to if they didn't want to, I guess.

Admiral Coye: No. In some respects, they were more fortunate. The ones that came in in 1934, they came in ahead of the Class of '34, so they really didn't lose any seniority, and they could be married. My class, '33, the ones who got their commission in 1933, couldn't get married for two years. I wasn't happy about that, because at the time, I was engaged to my present wife, and we would have liked to have gotten married in 1933, but we had to wait until 1935 to get married.

Q: Let's put her name on the record.

Admiral Coye: Her name is Elizabeth Gabriel. We all call her Betty Gabriel. As I mentioned earlier, we had our pictures from when I was five and she was four, but I didn't see her again until 1932, when her mother came down to Annapolis to visit my mother, who was living in Annapolis. My dad had died in 1931, and my mother had moved to Annapolis. So her mother came down with Betty to visit my mother, and that's when Betty and I met again.

Q: Did your love affair immediately start up?

Admiral Coye: Yes, almost immediately.

Q: I think that's rather quite fun and rather unusual, isn't it?

Admiral Coye: It is unusual.

Q: So you didn't get married; you had to wait those long two years.

Coye #1 - 12

Admiral Coye: We had to wait until 1935, yes.

Q: And did you request a particular assignment after you graduated, or were you simply assigned to the USS Northampton right out of the personnel office?

Admiral Coye: I don't remember whether we got a chance to request or not, but in any event, I went to the Northampton, which at that time was one of the newer heavy cruisers. I considered myself very fortunate to go to the Northampton, because it was a good ship, relatively new, and I had interesting duty on there. I went through the usual ensign's jobs. They tried to rotate you in various departments in engineering and gunnery and assistant navigator and things like that. It was an interesting assignment. It was based in Long Beach, but we did make a cruise in 1934 to the East Coast. When we went to the East Coast, they had a test to see how fast the fleet could get to the Panama Canal. I can remember going through the Panama Canal at nighttime at about 25 knots, which was really exciting.

Q: A little scary?

Admiral Coye: Yes.

Q: Where were you at the time? On the bridge?

Coye #1 - 13

Admiral Coye: Yes, I was on the bridge of the <u>Northampton</u>. This, as I say, was a test. At that time, we only had the one-ocean Navy, and they wanted to see how long it would take it to go from one ocean to the other.

Q: How long did it take? Do you remember?

Admiral Coye: No, I don't remember, but I remember the canal trip was very successful. Nobody ran aground.

Q: Or brushed the sides or anything?

Admiral Coye: No.

Q: That was Cruiser Division Four, I think.

Admiral Coye: Cruiser Division Four, yes.

Q: How many ships went through that exercise?

Admiral Coye: Well, all the battleships and all the cruisers from the West Coast went back to the East Coast. I can also remember going up to New York. We had a fleet review, and President Roosevelt reviewed the fleet. We spent some time in New York.

Coye #1 - 14

Q: Where was he when he reviewed it? Aboard what, do you remember?

Admiral Coye: I don't remember what he was aboard, no.

Q: An exciting experience.

Admiral Coye: An exciting experience, yes.

Q: According to my calculations, you would have had a normal tour aboard the Northampton of approximately two years or close to two years?

Admiral Coye: Yes, approximately two years. Actually, let's see, they had a program on there where they were short of aviators, and we had these scout planes on there, and so they would put nonaviators in to be aviation observers. I was assigned that job. While I enjoyed flying, I really didn't think it led to anything in the future, because my eyesight had gone down, and I couldn't pass the aviation physical for eyes. So I told them I wanted to go into submarines.

At that time, I applied for submarine school and there again, on the physical exam, the doctor found a hernia, and so I couldn't apply for submarines at that time. But in the meantime, while I was in the hospital ship, the Relief, recovering from the hernia operation (which in those days took 21 days; now it's about three days), I received orders to a new-construction destroyer, the Monaghan. I was very

Coye #1 - 15

pleased with that, because the Monaghan was being built back in the Boston Navy Yard, and my future wife lived in Massachusetts, at Worcester.

Q: That's kind of neat.

Admiral Coye: So I left the Northampton. As I recall, it was around March of '35. I went back to Boston and put the Monaghan in commission. The tour on the Monaghan was most interesting. This was one of the new 1,500-ton destroyers, the first ones that had been built since World War I. They called them the "gold-platers" because they were real fancy. We had high-pressure steam and more guns than the other ships, they were faster and just much more modern than the previous World War I destroyers. My skipper was Commander Thompson, who was a submarine officer and had been a skipper of an "L" boat in World War I—Commander R. R. Thompson.*

Since this was a new ship, we had lots of opportunities for unusual things. Our shakedown cruise was over to Northern Europe. I can remember we went to England, Belfast, Ireland. Even at that time in Northern Ireland there, they had barricades in the streets to separate the two Irish factions.

Q: The IRA and whatever they call the other one.

---

*Commander Robert R. Thompson, USN.

Coye #1 - 16

Admiral Coye: And this was in 1935, so that's been going on for a long time.

Q: Yes, it has.

Admiral Coye: Then we went to Copenhagen. It was an interesting cruise.

Q: Had you been to Europe before?

Admiral Coye: I had been to Europe on a midshipmen's cruise.

Q: Oh yes.

Admiral Coye: Also, we stopped at the island of Miquelon.

Q: That's a new name to me.

Admiral Coye: The Miquelon Islands are very interesting. They are up near Newfoundland, near Argentia. They are the last French North Atlantic colony. This was in 1935. Previous to that time, they had been very active in the rum-running business and had warehouses there full of liquor.

Q: Those were the days of Prohibition.

Admiral Coye: In the days of Prohibition. But the United States had concluded a treaty with France saying that they would no longer have this rum-running, and they'd sent a man up there to be a consul in the Miquelon Islands. The natives up there wouldn't let him stay; he came there and he asked for a place to stay and they said there's no room at any of the houses. So finally, the reason we were there was to establish a United States presence and make a goodwill trip.

Q: That was interesting and certainly different, wasn't it?

Admiral Coye: Certainly a different experience. These islands are just like being in France. All the people speak French, of course, and the fishing boats go back and forth between France and there. That keeps the population French. In any event, we went in there and at first they thought we were a revenue cutter, and they weren't very hospitable. But when they found out we weren't, they gave us a royal welcome. I remember they had all these warehouses full of champagne, and they gave us a big party, and they'd open a bottle of champagne and pour it in your glass. Then, if you wanted a refill, they wouldn't take the same bottle; they'd open another bottle. It was quite an event.

Q: I'll have to ask you if you could take it home with you.

Admiral Coye: No. Anyway, that was Isle de Miquelon. That was part

Coye #1 - 18

of our shakedown cruise. Also, since we were a new ship, they sent us down to the Mardi Gras in Mobile. Mobile had the oldest Mardi Gras in the United States.

Q: I didn't know that.

Admiral Coye: Yes, older than the New Orleans one. Since I was the junior officer on the <u>Monaghan,</u> when the mayor came aboard and said they needed a queen's escort, the captain said, "Jack, you be the queen's escort." It turned out that I went to all the official functions and sat in the reviewing stands and watched some of my senior officers lead the troops by. So that was very exciting.

Q: Were you married at this point?

Admiral Coye: I was married. I had protested, because we had some bachelors on there, like Jack Chew.* You probably know him; he was a bachelor at the time. But since I was the junior one, the captain said I would be the queen's escort, so I had to be the queen's escort. I don't know, this is sort of trivia.

Q: Oh, I think it's interesting.

---

*Lieutenant (junior grade) John L. Chew, USN, who eventually became a vice admiral.

Admiral Coye: Then later on we joined the fleet in the Monaghan, and we went down to South America to Callao. That's where we got the crossing the line ceremony.

Q: That's a new name to me.

Admiral Coye: Callao?

Q: Yes.

Admiral Coye: In Peru. Then we went back to the West Coast to San Diego. By this time my wife had driven out here and met me in San Diego. Shortly after that, we made a cruise up to Alaska and went through the inside passage. Our pilot at the time was Professor Farwell, who is an expert on rules of the road at sea and wrote quite a bit about them.* We went up there as a division, and I can remember going through there, and if it got foggy, why, he'd blow the whistle and we'd listen for the echoes for the whistle to see where we were. We went up to the Columbia Glacier and blew our whistle and watched chunks of ice come tumbling down.

I went for an airplane ride up there with a young fellow named Reeves, who has since had his own airline up there. I can remember the plane was similar to the Spirit of St. Louis. It was a Ryan,

---

*Lieutenant Commander Raymond F. Farwell, USNR, The Rules of the Nautical Road (Annapolis: U.S. Naval Institute, 1941).

but he had it on skis and this was in Valdez. He would land in the mudflats on skis, and then he'd land on the glaciers up on the ice. That was rather an interesting experience.

Q: I'm glad you liked it.

Admiral Coye: There's a picture of the Monaghan right there.

Q: I had in mind that you took the President Franklin Roosevelt on a fishing cruise in this period.

Admiral Coye: Oh yes. That's true. While we were on the Monaghan and before we joined the fleet, and since we were one of the newest destroyers, we were elected to take President Roosevelt on a fishing trip in the Bahamas. We went down to Fort Lauderdale where we picked up the President, and also they had the Presidential cutter, the Potomac. He didn't like it to be called the Presidential yacht, but the Presidential cutter was the Potomac, which had been a Coast Guard cutter. The ship had had quite a bit of modification before we took the President aboard. It had ramps aboard and things like that, because he was crippled. We had a very enjoyable fishing trip all around the Bahamas and West Indian Islands, the Tongue of the Ocean.

Q: What did you say?

Admiral Coye: The Tongue of the Ocean.

Q: The Tongue of the Ocean?

Admiral Coye: Yes, that's a very deep part of water down there.

Q: That's down near the Bahamas?

Admiral Coye: Near the Bahamas, yes. There were a few press aboard, as I recall. Whenever the President went fishing, why, when he came back, they took a picture of the President with a fish. No matter who caught the biggest fish, why, the one that the President was taken with was the biggest fish and that was the fish he caught.

Q: How did he get off and on the ship?

Admiral Coye: We lifted him off and on.

Q: With a crane?

Admiral Coye: No, we put him in the whaleboat and left him in the whaleboat and then lowered the whaleboat.

Q: Oh, I see.

Coye #1 - 22

Admiral Coye: He fished from a motor whaleboat.

Q: Oh, I see. But he went onto the whaleboat aboard ship which was then lifted into the water. I see. And then of course back up the same way.

Admiral Coye: Yes. I think that's how we did it.

Q: Those are bits of history that people aren't familiar with.

Admiral Coye: I guess we took him down the gangway, because it would have been more dangerous to have lowered him from the side of the ship, from the davit. I think we rigged the gangway and then carried him down the gangway. And then put him into the whaleboat. Then, after that, after we returned to Fort Lauderdale, the Presidental yacht, the Potomac, had to go back to Norfolk, and it was going to go back by itself. Since it had just been commissioned, it had only one officer on board. So they wanted to have another one. So, again, since I was the junior officer on the Monaghan, I got to ride the Presidential yacht from Lauderdale up to Norfolk.

Q: Was the President aboard?

Coye #1 - 23

Admiral Coye: No, he wasn't aboard. He went by train from Lauderdale to Washington.

Q: Your job we haven't actually mentioned. I think that's the first time—your assignment was assistant engineer aboard the Monaghan.

Admiral Coye: Yes.

Q: And that really went back to your early experience and things you did well at the Academy, and now you're having a chance to use it.

Admiral Coye: Right.

Q: And so then they asked you what you wanted to do next, and you said, "I want to go to ..."

Admiral Coye: Submarine school, yes. So I applied for submarine school and, as I say, my skipper on the Monaghan was a submariner, and he had recommended it. I thought I always wanted it, and in any event, so I applied and was accepted. I went to submarine school in January of 1937.

Q: For about six months?

Admiral Coye: Yes, a six-months course.

Coye #1 - 24

Q: Had you ever been aboard a submarine before?

Admiral Coye: Yes, at the Naval Academy they had an R-boat there one second-class summer. I had taken a short trip in that.

Q: You didn't get claustrophobia?

Admiral Coye: No.

Q: So you were there for six months. Do you want to tell me where submarine school is?

Admiral Coye: Yes, submarine school is in New London, Connecticut. I thoroughly enjoyed submarine school. I did well there for--I forget how many were in the class. I think there were about 25 or 30, and our assignments at the end of sub school were to be based on our class standings. I ended up, I think, standing number two.

Q: So number two isn't bad.

Admiral Coye: No. So I decided then that I wanted to go to the most modern submarine. We had our choice between the newer submarines which were based in San Diego or the S-boats in Panama or China or Honolulu or the R-boats in New London. Well, I decided I wanted to go to a new submarine and I went to the USS Shark, the SS-174, which was based in San Diego.

Q: Your assignment aboard the submarine was...

Admiral Coye: I was going to be engineer officer.

Q: You had a nice long tour on that.

Admiral Coye: Yes, I was on the Shark until 1940 or so.

Q: My dates say June 1937 til October 1940.

Admiral Coye: Yes.

Q: So that would have been more than the three years.

Admiral Coye: Yes, I was on the Shark quite a while. I learned a lot on the Shark. Being a new submarine, we had problems, mainly engineering problems. We were the first submarine to have the high-speed diesels, called Wintons, subsequently called General Motors diesels. The engines gave us a lot of problems, and the electrical generators gave us problems, and the motors gave us problems.

Q: It sounds like everything gave you problems!

Coye #1 - 26

Admiral Coye: Everything gave us problems, but fortunately we were able to solve those problems. My skipper, Captain C.J. Cater, was--at times I thought him a martinet, but actually, looking back, he was very capable.* He insisted that every little thing that went wrong be written up and reported back to the authorities back in Washington, everything that went wrong with these engines and generators and motors.

Q: Not to the manufacturer, but to BuShips?

Admiral Coye: We had what we called a "machinery casualty report." They were written up in meticulous detail as to what was wrong. Of course, it was up to Washington then to contact the manufacturers. I think largely as a result of this, the submarines that came on in World War II--that were built just prior to the war and during the war--had such good engineering performance because we, on the Shark, had pointed out the design deficiencies and they were corrected.

Q: You did that. You were the engineer, so you were responsible for that.

Admiral Coye: Yes, I did the hard work.

---
*Lieutenant Commander Charles J. Cater, USN.

Coye #1 - 27

Q: That must have given you some satisfaction.

Admiral Coye: It gave me a lot of satisfaction, yes, particularly later when everything was running good on the ships. But we did have a lot of problems on the Shark, and there were times when I wondered whether it was worth all the trouble, but it turned out it was.

Q: How many ships were in that category?

Admiral Coye: Basically, there were four. There was Porpoise, Pike, Shark, and Tarpon, which each had the same engineering plant. They each had the same problems that we did.

Q: Did you solve them for all four of them?

Admiral Coye: Well, we submitted more machinery casualty reports than the others did, and I think it was largely as a result of the Shark's problems that we got them all corrected in time for World War II.

Q: Before we go on, (I know I'm interrupting), but you were at sub school only six months. Was that long enough?

Admiral Coye: Yes, that was the normal course.

Q: I know, but it seems to me such a short time to learn all about

Coye #1 - 28

submarines.

Admiral Coye: No, I think it was was normal. I think it's about the same time as in Pensacola to learn to fly a plane. You can learn in Pensacola in about that time.

Q: But to me, I can relate an airplane to an automobile, but I can't relate a submarine to anything but a submarine.

Admiral Coye: Well, of course, you don't get your dolphins on graduating from submarine school. Once you go through submarine school, you go to your submarine, then you have to take a year, and you have to keep an extensive notebook and sketch the whole submarine and all the piping systems in it and demonstrate your ability to fire torpedoes and make dives and then have an examination by the division commander before you can get your dolphins.

Q: So that was just the beginning of the training.

Admiral Coye: That was the beginning of the training. As a matter of fact, the division commander who gave me my dolphins was Charlie Lockwood.* He was division commander then.

---

*Commander Charles A. Lockwood, Jr., USN, Commander Submarine Division 13. As a vice admiral, Lockwood was Commander Submarines Pacific Fleet during World War II.

Coye #1 - 29

Q: That wouldn't have been while you were an engineer, would it?

Admiral Coye: Yes.

Q: On board the Shark?

Admiral Coye: On board the Shark.

Q: And did you do all of that diving and shooting and charting and everything as an engineer?

Admiral Coye: Yes.

Q: I see. So you really knew your submarine by the time you...

Admiral Coye: Oh yes.

Q: Well, you had been there three years and some. It was really a good training period. On the job training, I guess.

Admiral Coye: Yes. Then after you get qualified in submarines, to wear the gold dolphins, then the next step is to get what they call "qualified in command." I also got that later on on the Shark.

Q: You qualified for command aboard the Shark.

Coye #1 - 30

Admiral Coye: Yes.

Q: You said the Shark was in San Diego. Its home port was San Diego.

Admiral Coye: Yes. The Shark was in San Diego. Then it transferred out to Honolulu in 1938. It was transferred out to Squadron Four out there. It had been Squadron Six in San Diego and then went out to Honolulu and became in Squadron Four. We operated out of there.

The most unusual incident, I guess, was when the Yorktown, a carrier, ran over us and collided with us. It was during an exercise with them. They had written out an operation order telling the submarine exactly what to do, what depths to be at, when to come up and show its periscope, when to go deep, when to turn. We were following out the instructions in detail, but unfortunately the operation order did not specify exactly what the carrier was supposed to do. The carrier stopped its screws and then made a turn toward us, and when we came up, when we were supposed to, to show the periscope, why, all the skipper could see was gray paint. He immediately ordered us to go deep. I was the diving officer at the time. But before we could get deep, why, it knocked off the shears of the submarine at the bridge level.

Q: All topside?

Admiral Coye: Yes.

Q: Would that be the conning tower, even?

Admiral Coye: It didn't knock the conning tower, but just above the conning tower.

Q: I see.

Admiral Coye: And also the radio trunk where the antenna goes up—that has a porcelain insulator on it—and it knocked that off, and that started to flood one compartment, the forward battery compartment. We started to go down, but fortunately we were able to control it and blow the ballast tanks and surfaced. But we had taken quite a bit of water in the forward battery.

Q: Does that water in the batteries do a lot of chemical reaction?

Admiral Coye: Well, it generates chlorine gas.

Q: That's what I was afraid of.

Admiral Coye: But in any event, that was one of the first board of investigations that I had been an interested party in, since I was the diving officer. But I ended up getting a letter of commendation out of it for getting the submarine back up to the surface.

Coye #1 - 32

Q: Well, it was a pretty shaking experience, wasn't it?

Admiral Coye: It was a shaking experience.

Q: It was a real literal shaking of the submarine.

Admiral Coye: Oh yes.

Q: Terrible.

Admiral Coye: Yes.

Q: How long did this up-and-down take you, an hour?

Admiral Coye: Oh no. We came up right away; right on the other side of the carrier, we popped up.

Q: I see.

Admiral Coye: Because I had started to blow almost as soon as we started heading down. I could see that we weren't able to control it with just the planes. The boat was getting heavy, and so I started to blow ballast right away and we were able to get it up to surface.

Q: I hope someone on the Yorktown was given a disciplinary letter.

Were they?

Admiral Coye: I don't remember. I think later. I can't remember his name, but I know the skipper of the Yorktown later made admiral.

Q: Well, maybe it wasn't too serious. Was the commendation generally because of the way you handled it and kept it from being a disaster?

Admiral Coye: Yes, right. And the fact that we had gotten the submarine up to the surface when it was flooding and taking on a lot of water.

Q: I'm awful glad you did. Aren't you?

Admiral Coye: Yes. I'll never forget that date. It was September 9th, 1940. At one time I figured I've been living on borrowed time ever since.

Q: Oh. I think people are lucky. There are people who are lucky, and you are a lucky man.

Admiral Coye: Yes.

Q: Not that you didn't have the skill.

Coye #1 - 34

Admiral Coye: Yes.

Q: So now tell me more about the USS Shark. You went out to Honolulu, you said, in 1938.

Admiral Coye: 1938.

Q: And so you were there another year and a half at least.

Admiral Coye: Yes. We did the usual things in Honolulu. I can remember we went on what we called "readiness for war trials."

Q: War games?

Admiral Coye: War games, yes. We had the fleet war games, and we had our own exercises--readiness for war trials, is what they called them--in which you went out and you had to spend so many hours at full power and you had to spend so many hours at dives. Always one of our problems was you had to make fresh water. I can remember that. You didn't have very good evaporators. One of the things was that you had to have as much water in your tanks when you came back as you had when you left. That was always the biggest problem in the readiness for war trials.

Q: Did you ever do any of these war games that related to Japanese and action against them?

Admiral Coye: Yes. One of the fleet problems out there (I forget the year), of course they always designated one fleet as the "blue fleet" and one as the "orange fleet." It seems to me that we were normally part of the "orange fleet" attacking the battleships and things like that.

Q: You were the Japanese. You were the bad guys?

Admiral Coye: We were the bad guys, as I remember it, yes.

Q: Did you win?

Admiral Coye: No, I think they had it rigged so we would always lose.

Q: Psychologically.

Admiral Coye: Yes.

Q: Interesting. So you learned a great deal about submarines during the tour, I guess.

Admiral Coye: Yes, I did.

Coye #1 - 36

Q: And you got your dolphins and you qualified as commanding officer in that period of time.

Admiral Coye: Yes.

Q: Are we overlooking anything?

Admiral Coye: I don't think so, no. The second skipper was Phil Compton, and he was an outstanding submarine officer.* He later had physical problems and had to retire, but he was an exceptional officer, and I learned a lot from him.

Q: That is good, I think, in the Navy. Many times people, nowadays, people have the aspect of the military as, "Oh, well..." but frankly, my experience in the Navy (and I'm sure you'll agree with me) is that it is the most wonderful learning experience in all fields.

Admiral Coye: That's right, and you learn from all your individual skippers and bosses. You pick up something from each of them, I think. Some of them have their bad points, but you learn not to emulate that, just good things.

I remember one skipper, going back to the Northampton, just before I came on there he had been relieved, but he could name every man in

---

*Lieutenant Commander Philip D. Compton, USN.

that crew and call them by name.

Q: The enlisted men, you mean?

Admiral Coye: The enlisted men. And there were over 600 men.

Q: That's hard to believe.

Admiral Coye: Yes. If he saw a man that he hadn't seen before, he'd ask him his name and the next time he'd see him, he's say, "Good morning, Jones," or whatever his name was.

Q: I never have heard that.

Admiral Coye: It was a skill. Like some people can play cards and know all the cards in the deck. He knew all the sailors on the ship. And they loved him for it, of course.

Q: Of course.

Admiral Coye: But I never could do that. I would try, of course, with smaller crews. In destroyers and submarines, you could pretty much do it, but once I got on a bigger ship I couldn't do it.

Q: I just never heard of that.

Coye #1 - 38

Admiral Coye: Walter Vernou was his name, yes.*

Q: I never heard of a man having that. I've heard fantastic things of remembering people over the years, all kinds of stories. But to be able to remember the name of every man in the crew is incredible.

Admiral Coye: Yes. Now, where are we?

Q: We were both agreeing that there are many things you learn in the Navy that the military isn't given credit for teaching, like personnel, administration, besides the technical and mechanical things and command. There's just a great deal to be learned. I probably sound naive or childish, because they say that probably everybody knows that, but I think that in this day and age, when the military comes under some sort of criticism or not given the benefit that it should, I resent it.

Admiral Coye: I agree.

Q: So shall we leave the Shark?

Admiral Coye: Yes, I think we've covered the Shark pretty well.

---

*Captain Walter N. Vernou, USN, who soon afterward became a flag officer.

Coye #1 - 39

Q: Well, you accomplished a great deal on that. So then you went from there to another submarine that was being recommissioned, as I recall.

Admiral Coye: Yes, I went to the R-18, which was one of the R-class submarines, which had been built in World War I. It had been decommissioned and laid up in the Philadelphia Navy Yard in about 1934 or 1935. I don't remember the exact date. It was sort of a rusting hulk when I joined it. I was the first officer to go to the R-18, and I remember I had a very small crew—a yeoman and a couple of the men that were going to be in the prospective crew. The yard was overhauling it.

Of course at that time we wanted to get the ship in commission, because if you weren't attached to a commissioned submarine, you weren't getting any submarine pay. So even though I think with only about a half a dozen of us, myself and about five or six men, we decided we would commission this ship. So I went up to the commandant of the yard, and he made me sign a slip of paper saying I had received one submarine and we hoisted the flag on it and commissioned it. We started drawing submarine pay.

The rest of the crew came, and most of the crew were people who had been recalled from the Fleet Reserve. I remember we had one of the chiefs who had been on one of the K-boats which predated World War I. He had been out of the Navy for a good 15 years, and that's the kind of people that we were getting, plus some raw recruits that had

Coye #1 - 40

never even been to submarine school. So this was quite a job getting this submarine organized.

I was ordered as executive officer. The skipper came shortly after that; that was E.J. MacGregor.* Then we got one other officer fresh out of submarine school, and we only had three officers on it when we left the navy yard to go to New London. As I say, it was an old submarine, and it was really a pile of rust, but we managed to get it running and operating.

Q: Did it function in all it was supposed to do? Could it dive?

Admiral Coye: It dived.

Q: Weren't you scared?

Admiral Coye: Yes, we dived it to its test depth, which was 200 feet. We got back up all right. There was another submarine there about the same time; one of the O-boats made its test dive to 200 feet, and it didn't come back up.

Q: What was the name of that?

Admiral Coye: It was either the O-8 or O-12. But anyway, I

---

*Lieutenant Edgar J. MacGregor III, USN.

remember going to paint the bilges back in the motor room, and they were chipping away to get the rust off, and the chipping hammer went right through the hull. It was really not in very good shape.

Q: I would think that's an understatement.

Admiral Coye: Yes. We got it operating. It had the old what we called "Nelseco" engines in it—big, heavy engines. The thrill on those was that normally you started them by connecting the motors to them and turned them over and then gave them the throttle to start them, but technically they were supposed to be able to start on air and making what was called an "air start" which was really quite a thrill, because usually smoke would come out and sometimes it would start and sometimes it wouldn't.

Q: I hope you're on the surface when this happens.

Admiral Coye: Oh yes, you're on the surface when this happens. In any event, we got the boat out of the navy yard and up to New London. Then they ordered us down to Panama to Coco Solo Submarine Base. We made a trip down there. We did have some engine problems, because I remember part of the time being on the end of a towline from the tender that went down with us. But we got to Panama.

Then we operated out of Panama. Our operating areas were in the Pacific side, so to get to them we had to go from Coco Solo (which is

Coye #1 - 42

on the Atlantic side), through the canal, and we went through the canal quite a few times. We'd go over the Pacific side for maybe two weeks operating and then come back to Coco Solo. So we got very familiar with the canal.

Q: Can you tell me what time we are talking about? I know you went to the navy yard in January of 1941. Was all this that you are describing during the year of 1941?

Admiral Coye: Yes, I think this was all during '41.

Q: Because I'm getting up to where was your ship on December the seventh?

Admiral Coye: Yes, this was all in 1941. I had joined the R-18 in 1940, hadn't I?

Q: I had understood it was January the eighth, so it was the end of 1940, the beginning of 1941.

Admiral Coye: Yes. We went down to Panama, and then we came back from Panama. They had decided that they were going to give the R-boats to England.

Q: Good idea.

Coye #1 - 43

Admiral Coye: Yes. So they brought us back from Panama, and we got to the States, up to New London, as I recall, around September or October of 1941. At this time, Betty was pregnant with my boy, the second child, and the doctor wouldn't allow her to leave Panama, because she was having problems hanging onto the baby. So she stayed on down in Panama. I came up with the boat to New London. Then we operated furnishing services to the submarine school, and I think by this time we had the neutrality patrol, and we would run targets for the destroyers up off Casco Bay. I can remember doing that.

Q: Weren't you commanding officer by this time?

Admiral Coye: Let me see. I took command there. I can't remember the exact dates.

Q: I see here that you were commanding officer there for about a year.

Admiral Coye: Yes.

Q: When did you become commanding officer?

Admiral Coye: In April of 1942. As I say, we had been in New London. On December 7th of 1941, we were in New London. Actually, my wife had just arrived from Panama. She was on the last ship that left Panama to New York. I forget the name of the ship. She arrived in New York

Coye #1 - 44

December 6th.

Q: Can you remember your reactions and the reactions of everybody there besides being crazy on that day?

Admiral Coye: Yes.

Q: Did it affect you personally in your command and your leadership?

Admiral Coye: The baby was very sick and so we subsequently, within a week, had to have what is called a pyloric stenosis operation. So I was probably more concerned with the baby than I was with the fact that a war had started. There was not too much that we could do around New London to fight the Japanese.

Q: Of course not. Did your ship go to the British?

Admiral Coye: No. Once we had entered the war, the United States decided they would have to keep these submarines. So then they used us for patrolling off the Atlantic Coast looking for German submarines. We would make patrols. We first started out in New London, and they gave us an area off the coast there, because by this time the German submarines were starting to sink ships right off the Atlantic Coast, and hopefully we would be able to catch the German submarines on the surface and sink them.

Coye #1 - 45

Later on (I'm getting a little ahead of myself), we made several patrols, I think a good half dozen. They were short patrols of about two weeks' duration, because that's about all we could stand on living in an R-boat, because we didn't have any air-conditioning like the modern submarines have, and you didn't carry much fresh water. You couldn't take a bath and you just barely had enough fresh water to brush your teeth with. They were small and cramped, and we usually had extra people aboard, because we were training them to go and get qualified and get training so they could man the newer submarines that were coming out. The normal crew of an R-boat would be maybe 25 people, and we were carrying usually 35 or 40. So we were crowded.

Q: What was the safety of the boat at that time? Had you put it in shape so that it really was a safe operating boat?

Admiral Coye: For a boat that was that old, it was probably safe. As I say, it had a test depth of 200 feet, and we never tried it any deeper than that. It could shoot torpedoes. It carried four torpedoes forward, Mark 10 torpedoes, and we had a couple of reloads. So, as I recall, it carried either 8 or 12 total torpedoes. It was a simple submarine, and it was a good little submarine.

Later on, I took command in April of 1942, and then we went to Bermuda to be our base. We were still going to hunt out German submarines, and probably the scariest incident I had during the war happened on a trip to Bermuda. We were just approaching the island of

Coye #1 - 46

Bermuda, and a friendly Navy plane bombed us, and it did quite a bit of damage.

Q: Were you on the surface?

Admiral Coye: We were on the surface. This was bright and early in the morning, just before dawn. We were in what they called a submarine sanctuary. A submarine sanctuary is supposed to be a safe zone for submarines, and the airplanes aren't supposed to bomb anybody in it. But this pilot didn't get the word and saw us, and when we saw him coming in, actually we had an American flag tied to the periscope, and we fired the recognition signal. But since he still was coming in, I dove. And as we were diving, he dropped bombs on us, and it turned out that it flooded the forward trim tank, and of course all the lights and everything went out and the circuit breakers all went out. On the depth gauge the needles fell off that. We were in bad shape there for a few moments. But then we did manage to level off and came up to periscope depth and looked around. The plane was still flying, so I stayed there and we were scheduled to meet an escort. This was just outside of Bermuda, and about an hour or so later, we saw the escort and surfaced right alongside the escort. But back at the base, they had more or less given us up. They thought the plane had sunk us, because this same pilot (and I really don't remember his name) had sighted a German submarine a few days before and he hadn't attacked it. So he was ...

Coye #1 - 47

Q: He was bound to attack something.

Admiral Coye: When he saw a submarine, he was going to attack. Actually, it turned out he was the wing man. There were two planes and he was the wing man. The senior pilot, who was a classmate of mine and I've also forgotten his name, I hadn't told him we were out there. But anyway, it was fortunate that we got through that. That was probably the closest experience I had during the war.

Q: When you say that is hard to---of course, it's terrible, but to think of all the other experiences you had in the Pacific, it's incredible that you were almost sunk by our own forces. Was it Navy or Air Force?

Admiral Coye: Navy.

Q: A Navy pilot, too!

Admiral Coye: Then again, we had a board of investigation on it and I was an interested party and I got another letter of commendation.

Q: Well worth it, well worth it, but a scary incident. Were you in command at the time?

Admiral Coye: I was in command, yes.

Coye #1 - 48

Q: Even that early in the morning?

Admiral Coye: Yes.

Q: What were your hours? Were you in command the whole time?

Admiral Coye: No, you're always in command.

Q: I know you were in command, but I mean where were you literally?

Admiral Coye: I think I was on the bridge. Yes, I was on the bridge, because we only had three officers, so I took the watch. We were approaching Bermuda, and I wanted to be up there to sight it.

Q: And you remember full well seeing that airplane. I'm sure you remember it.

Admiral Coye: Yes, I remember that.

Q: So, you've had several lucky escapes now, the first of many.

Admiral Coye: To go back a little bit, I was also on the R-18 when I was in Panama. When I was executive officer, I was also navigator. We had a board of investigation because the R-18 had gone through the minefields off the Atlantic Coast, off Coco Solo. We had gone through

Coye #1 - 49

twice, and these were mines that could be set off from shore, an Army minefield. The second time we did it, they called a board of investigation.

Q: Weren't you supposed to?

Admiral Coye: No, you weren't supposed to go through the minefield.

Q: Did you know they were there?

Admiral Coye: We knew they were there, and there was a path that you were supposed to take to go through there.

Q: To clear, yes.

Admiral Coye: And we showed in this board of investigtion that if we followed the instructions that they put out, that you were bound to go right through the minefield. Because we had been following the instructions perfectly, and we went through the minefield.

Q: Put out by the Army.

Admiral Coye: Yes, the Army and somebody else down there. I forget. The Naval Control of Shipping. It was about three activities involved in this thing. That was part of the fault. In any event, I was an

Coye #1 - 50

interested party in that board of investigation. I also got a letter of commendation for that for proving that...

Q: I think they felt that the fact that you were still alive entitled you to a letter of commendation. I'm teasing you, of course.

Admiral Coye: Yes. I had almost forgotten about that. Okay, where are we now?

Q: Well, we're going to go back to the prospective commanding officer's school.

Admiral Coye: Let's see. I had a little more on the R-18. We spent some time in Bermuda; we made patrols looking out for German submarines. We never did see any. Then they ordered us down to Trinidad to run target for the escorts for the convoys from Trinidad up along the coast. They were mainly running bauxite from up there. So we spent about two months, as I recall it, in Trinidad, running target services. Then we came back around Christmastime. This would be in 1942. We came back to New London. I think that about covers the 18 boat.

Q: And then you went right in New London to the prospective commanding officers' school?

Admiral Coye: Yes.

Q: Even though you qualified as commanding officer some years before, this was a school just for prospective commanding officers?

Admiral Coye: Yes, this was called PCO school. It was inaugurated in World War II, and they concentrated primarily on firing torpedoes. They had brought back some of the early skippers. I remember one was Bart Bacon, I think, who was in charge of the school.* They would give you the benefit of their experiences on war patrols in the Pacific. We would concentrate on making practice torpedo approaches, both in the attack teacher, which is a land-based thing in which you look at models of ships and things like that, and also running submarines out in Long Island Sound. You'd practice making approaches and firing torpedoes. It was mostly on how to make torpedo approaches, both daytime approaches and night approaches.

Q: What kind of submarines did you have to practice with?

Admiral Coye: The main ones we used were the Marlin and the Mackerel. The Marlin and the Mackerel were small submarines, not as big as a fleet submarine, but they were new submarines and they had the same torpedo data computer that fleet boats, the newer submarines, had.

---
*Commander Barton E. Bacon, Jr., USN, who had been in command of the USS Pickerel.

Coye #1 - 52

They were excellent for their purpose. They had been designed as a small submarine, but when it turned out we needed the range for the war in Japan, they weren't suitable for that, because they didn't have the range. But they were modern submarines.

Q: What kind of torpedoes did you use?

Admiral Coye: We used Mark 14 torpedoes.

Q: Real ones?

Admiral Coye: Real ones, but instead of having an explosive warhead, where the warhead was it was filled with what was called an exercise head. It was filled with water, and it had a device that at the end of the torpedo run the water would get blown out and the torpedo would float to the surface and they'd recover it and use it over again.

Q: I wanted to get into the problems with the torpedoes, but I don't think this is the right place to do it yet. How long were you at PCO school? Not too long, I think.

Admiral Coye: Not too long.

Q: A month?

Coye #1 - 53

Admiral Coye: It wasn't over a month. It might have been only three weeks. It was three to four weeks.

Q: I show that you left the R-18 in about April of 1943, and then you were out in the Pacific in June of 1943. So there wasn't much time in between there.

Admiral Coye: No, it was probably a three- to four-week course, as I remember it. It was only a small class—maybe five or six in the class. This was just to train prospective skippers. Then from there they sent you out either to Honolulu or Australia or someplace to take command of a boat in the war zone.

Q: And you knew that's where you were going and that's what you were going to do?

Admiral Coye: Yes.

Q: Did you know where you were going at the time? When you got your orders, you knew, but was that it?

Admiral Coye: No, I was ordered to Brisbane, Australia, and I flew out there. I flew out, I remember, in Pan Am from San Francisco to Honolulu and then they had Pan Am then flying what had been PBMs from Honolulu to Brisbane. We stopped at Johnston and Fiji and it was quite a flight out there.

Q: It's a long, long trip.

Admiral Coye: Yes, it's a long trip.

Q: Can you describe on the tape which part of Australia is Brisbane?

Admiral Coye: Brisbane is on the east coast of Australia.

Q: How far?

Admiral Coye: About halfway up; it's north of Sydney, but it's about halfway up the eastern coast of Australia.

Q: Can you try to describe for me the commodore who was in charge and the command and describe the parameters, something of what Brisbane looked like in those days?

Admiral Coye: Oh well, let's see. We had a tender there. As I recall, it was the <u>Fulton</u>, and it was at New Farm Wharf, which is just a wharf in Brisbane. The commodore was Jimmy Fife.[*] He was assigned so many submarines to operate. I think it was Task Force 72, and he

---

[*]Rear Admiral James Fife, Jr., USN, Commander Task Force 72.

had a staff and, of course, the overhaul facilities with the Fulton was a dry dock there that they could dock submarines. Normally they kept one squadron there at that time, but occasionally if any of those submarines were lost, why, they'd be replaced temporarily with boats from Honolulu. The majority of our submarines were based in Pearl. They were based in Brisbane and also on the western coast of Australia in Perth. I never did get to Perth. But anyhow, for a while there, when I first got to Brisbane, I was on the staff of Commodore Fife, just waiting for a job, and I was sort of assistant operations officer. John Murphy was the operations officer.* So I got to learn a lot about what the submarines were doing and what areas they were going to and to study their patrol reports and talk with the people. Just in general, I got the feel of the area and what the submarines were doing.

Q: What was the name of his force? I have Submarine Command, South Pacific Force. Is that correct?

Admiral Coye: I'm sure that's the full name of it.

Q: And you called it...

Admiral Coye: Task Force 72 is normally what we called ourselves. Task Force 71 was Perth, and Task Force 72 was Brisbane.

---

*Commander John W. Murphy, Jr., USN.

Coye #1 - 56

Q: Were there any conflicts between the Army and the Navy and those sort of things which one hears about in other times and places? There were conflicts in the command structure.

Admiral Coye: Well, there probably was, but at that time I was down in a real low echelon.

Q: You were a lieutenant commander?

Admiral Coye: I was a lieutenant commander, right. I wasn't really worrying about the conflicts between the admirals and the generals.

Q: Okay.

Admiral Coye: I have some criticism later on, if you want to discuss it, of the way the generals were employing the submarines.

Q: Was that at this period? You tell me when it should come in.

Admiral Coye: I'll tell you later, yes.

Q: Okay.

Admiral Coye: As I say, I was in the operations office of Commodore Fife, awaiting assignment to command a submarine. Normally what happened was that a prospective commanding officer went out for one patrol with one of the regular submarines. This was called a PCO patrol. However, at that time they were a little short of skippers in Brisbane, and while I had been scheduled to go out on a patrol, why, it turned out that I didn't have to go as a prospective commanding officer, but I went directly as skipper of the Silversides. I was very fortunate to get the Silversides, because it was a fairly new submarine and had been commissioned, as I recall, in December of 1941. It had a good record, and it had a really fine skipper in Creed Burlingame and had made five excellent patrols.[*] So I considered myself to be really fortunate to get ordered to get to command the Silversides.

Q: You are quoted as saying he was a hard act to follow.

Admiral Coye: Yes, he was. He was a dynamic leader, and the crew all loved him. Of course they didn't know me, but I made up my mind that this was a successful submarine and that if we were to continue, that I would try to mold myself to the way the crew was doing things. So the first patrol, I didn't change very much of the routine at all; I kept up the routine that had been established and I was fortunate in having a good executive officer in Bob Worthington, Class of 1938.[**]

---

[*]Lieutenant Commander Creed C. Burlingame, USN.
[**]Lieutenant Robert K. Worthington, USN.

Coye #1 - 58

Bob had made all the previous patrols, not as exec, but he had put the ship in commission and he knew the ship well. He has a brilliant mind; he stood number four in his class of 1938. He was real sharp on manning the torpedo data computer, which usually makes or breaks you as to whether you are going to get hits or not with torpedoes. All in all, it was very fortunate.

Q: I think it's remarkable that you went on your first patrol, as I would say, "just cold," without having had any indoctrination on this, at least on this particular submarine.

Admiral Coye: Well, as I say, I considered myself very fortunate, because they did have a shortage of skippers there at Brisbane, and they needed one, and I was there and I got the job.

Q: Again, your luck was holding, right?

Admiral Coye: My luck was holding, yes. Well, let's see. We got away for the sixth patrol on the 21st of July of 1943.

Q: Is this the sixth patrol of the ship or ...

Admiral Coye: It's the sixth patrol of the ship which was my ...

Q: Your first patrol?

Admiral Coye: My first patrol.

Q: Okay.

Admiral Coye: We headed up north along the eastern coast of Australia, and on the way to patrol areas we had a submarine rescue vessel called the Coucal which acted as target. We made practice approaches on her. We also had two other submarines with us, the Tuna and the Growler. So we all conducted practice approaches. Then on the 27th of July, we topped off our fuel from the Coucal, and from there we left to go to our area. We had to go up past Guadalcanal and between Green Islands. We were going to patrol in an area just south of Truk. On this patrol, we had quite a few good contacts.

The first attack we made on this patrol was on the 2nd of August when we sighted a seaplane tender, I believe it was, that was running unescorted. Now, this was unusual for a ship to go unescorted. But anyhow, we sighted her early in the morning, around 7:00 o'clock and dove and made a good approach on them, and we had them. We fired four torpedoes. Of course, at that time, I was fresh out of PCO school, and I really was good with practice at firing torpedoes, and it was a good shot. However, two of the torpedoes prematured. A premature is when a torpedo goes off by itself. Usually it takes about 300 yards for it to arm and then at 300 yards it will go bang all by itself. They had been having trouble with torpedo exploders--all the submarines had. We were taking out a new batch of exploders that had been modified to make them more sensitive. The original Mark 6 exploder was a magnetic exploder, and theoretically you set it to go underneath the ship, and as it crossed underneath the ship, it went off and due to the magnetism of the ship, it broke the ship's back, and the ship sank.

Well, they had been having problems that they weren't exploding when they went underneath the ship, so they had sent out from BuOrd a couple of experts and they modified the torpedoes, and we took out the first batch of torpedoes, one of the first batches that had been modified to make them more sensitive.* Well, as it subsequently turned out, they made them so sensitive that if the torpedo depth control wasn't perfect, if it would wiggle a little bit, then that would destroy the magnetic field and that torpedo would explode. They found that out later.

But anyhow, this target was an ideal target. Two of the torpedoes prematured, and this gave, of course, our position away, and the target saw these and radically maneuvered and avoided the other two torpedoes. We had fired a total of four torpedoes on them.

The second attack in this patrol was again against an unescorted large target which, from its appearance, looked like a naval auxiliary, maybe a submarine tender. Actually, he was going from Truk to Rabaul, and he was going fairly fast. We were in ideal position. When we picked them up, we were dead ahead of them. We

---

*BuOrd—Bureau of Ordnance.

dove and got in excellent position to make the torpedo attack. I simply pulled off the track and fired four stern tubes at them in a good firing range of about 2,000 yards. The torpedoes should have hit. However, looking through the periscope, I saw two of the torpedoes premature just this side of the target. Of course, this alerted them, and the other two torpedoes missed him. I read later in an intelligence report that the target had sighted these torpedoes and that they did premature. They prematured just maybe 30 or 40 yards from the side of the ship. The target, of course, went on undamaged.

Q: Was the problem of the premature torpedoes solved?

Admiral Coye: Well, later on they inactivated the magnetic feature of the exploder. This had been a sore point for many months, because the torpedoes had been designed to fire on magnetism, and theoretically one torpedo would break the ship's back and it would sink it, but the magnetic exploders were not working, or they were working too well and prematuring. So what eventually they did was to inactivate the magnetic feature of the torpedoes, and then you set the torpedo depth shallower, and the torpedoes were supposed to explode on contact with the side of the ship.

Q: I'm sure that having them go and having a good target and a good shot and having them premature was completely debilitating to the crew.

Admiral Coye: Oh yes. Of course, it not only gave your position away and it not only didn't sink any ships, but it was bad for morale—and this was a problem which, as someone has said, if we had had good torpedoes in the first couple of years of the war, why, the war would have been over a year earlier. People have said that.

Q: It took that long to solve the problem—two years?

Admiral Coye: Oh yes, and at this point the problem is not yet solved, because later on when we were setting them to fire on contact, we found that if you took the ideal shot and hit the target 90 degrees (that is, what we call a 90 track, hit it right abeam), this would deform the contact exploder, and they wouldn't go off. There are numerous examples of this. I can remember getting the message out on patrol (this is somewhat later) to try to hit them at an oblique angle or set them to run so that they hit on the turn of the bilge. Well, of course, this is pretty difficult to know where the turn of the bilge is, and odds are the torpedo isn't going to run at its exact set depth anyway.

So that problem was later solved, I guess, about sometime in 1944 when they replaced the firing pin of the contact exploder. Instead of a steel pin, they put in a light pin out of aluminum, and this did not deform when the torpedo hit the side of the ship. Then we were getting good torpedoes, but by this time, it was 1944. There is a lot of material on this. You'll find it in Clay Blair's book <u>Silent</u>

Victory.*

Q: So now we're still on your first patrol. How many torpedoes did you expend without hits on your first patrol? What was the number you said?

Admiral Coye: On our first patrol we fired 14 torpedoes and didn't get any hits. At least four were seen to premature, so actually we didn't sink any ships on that first patrol, unfortunately.

Q: I'll bet you were disappointed.

Admiral Coye: Oh, I was greatly disappointed and when we got back in, see---we carried 24 torpedoes. They closely examined the ten remaining torpedoes to check the exploders, and they wanted to check to make sure that our torpedomen had not done anything to them. They found that we hadn't violated any of the principles. We hadn't touched the exploders. The exploders were as they were given to us.

Q: So it was the fault of the torpedo and not any of you or your crew.

Admiral Coye: Right. As I say, we had one other attack there in that

---

*Clay Blair, Jr., Silent Victory: The U.S. Submarine War Against Japan (Philadelphia: J.P. Lippincott Company, 1975).

Coye #1 - 64

patrol and that was all misses too.

Q: And you returned, after your first patrol, to Brisbane?

Admiral Coye: We returned, after our first patrol, to Brisbane. We returned on the 12th of September. Do you want to figure out the days? I don't remember.

Q: I had figured that you were gone on your first patrol about 53 days.

Admiral Coye: That's about right, yes. We left on the 21st of July, and we returned on the 12th of September of 1943.

Q: That's a long time, isn't it?

Admiral Coye: Well, yes. That wasn't our longest patrol, though. But it was a long time. Your normal patrol was that you left your base, and you went to your assigned area and you spent 30 days in the area and you came back. Depending on how far the area was, why, it usually worked out to 50 or 60 days total. Of course, if you fired all your torpedoes, then you got to come back early. That was always a good thing to do that. We did that later on in three of our patrols.

Q: I was interested in what the usual patrol was. I was interested also in the use of intelligence reports and how that related to the deployments and did the people in Admiral Fife's staff—how did they go about deciding about where you would go?

Admiral Coye: Well, of course, Admiral Fife had a certain assigned area of the ocean to work in, and he was getting intelligence reports, and he had so many submarines that he could put in the areas. He'd put them where he thought they most likely would make contact. As you know, we were getting some intelligence—the Ultras were giving us good information, though they varied from time to time. When the Japanese would change their codes, the Ultra information was missing or not that good. As we used to say, the time to go on patrol was in the light of the Ultras and in the dark of the moon, because we didn't like going out on a bright moonlight night.

Q: Ultra means ultra-secret, I believe.

Admiral Coye: Ultra means ultra-secret, yes.

Q: And where did those come from?

Admiral Coye: Oh, they were people who were breaking the codes.

Q: But in Washington?

Admiral Coye: Some of them were in Washington and some of them were in Pearl Harbor. I think there were probably a few of them down in Australia there too---units. Of course we were purposely not told much about how they got the information, in the event of course that any of the people were captured, they didn't want them divulging the fact that we were breaking their codes. When we did get a message that had Ultra information, why, only the captain and perhaps the executive officer (who was navigator) were supposed to be able to read that message. It was very closely held.

Q: Would your area change, perhaps, as a result of an Ultra message after you had left for your patrol?

Admiral Coye: Yes. Commodore Fife could deploy you wherever he wanted to, and he could change your area, yes. He sent us, I think, almost daily messages with information. Of course, we didn't answer too much, because submarines normally kept radio silence because we didn't want the Japanese to be using their direction finders on us. It was unusual for a submarine just to use its radio just to say something that wasn't extra important. If you had made a contact and you hadn't been able to sink the contact, that was an excuse to come up and tell the authority about it so that maybe he could get other submarines that could get in position to do it. But for just ordinary things, you didn't use your radio at all.

Q: You talked about your first patrol, but I don't believe we've identified your operating area.

Admiral Coye: The operating area was in general between Truk and Rabaul. Part of that time we spent on a scouting line south of Truk. This was whenever General MacArthur's forces were making a move for another landing, why, he would have the submarines put on a scouting line south of Truk so that if any of the Japanese battle fleet came out of Truk toward wherever he was making the landing, that he would get word of this.* Of course, this kept the submarines more or less stationary. We were running back and forth on the surface. Usually, I think we were about 30 miles apart, and he would employ maybe half a dozen submarines to do this. This meant that you weren't free to be chasing convoys; you were more or less stationary, though Admiral Fife would try to move it 10 or 20 miles every day north or south. But it was a very frustrating experience, because you were tied to a single line that you had to be on and it meant that you weren't making contact with merchant ships at all or convoys.

Q: Which you thought really was your primary purpose.

Admiral Coye: Which was our purpose, and of course General MacArthur, I'm sure, had good intelligence and would have known if the Japanese

---
*General Douglas MacArthur, AUS, Supreme Allied Commander, Southwest Pacific.

fleet were coming down. It wasn't exactly a waste of submarine capabilities, but it was not the best employment for them.

Later on, they Japanese, as a matter of fact, had the same principle. They would deploy their submarines on a scouting line when we were about to make an attack someplace, and we got word of this and we went down that scouting line and we sank every one of the Japanese subs, just pinged on them, and we knew about where they were and that there would be another one in 20 or 30 miles away. I think the prime example was the USS England which sank, I think it was, three submarines in maybe one day or so.* So this was not a good employment.

Q: It's complete vulnerability for anyone who foresaw what was happening.

Admiral Coye: Yes.

Q: Now when these Japanese submarines were shot, you said that was by a destroyer?

Admiral Coye: Yes, a DE, I think it was, the USS England, as I remember the name. There were other ones that sank, too, but the

---

*For a firsthand account by the ship's executive officer, see Captain John A. Williamson (with William D. Lanier), "The Twelve Days of the England," U.S. Naval Institute Proceedings, March 1980, pages 76-83.

Coye #1 - 69

England was the prime example of how to sink Japanese submarines when they were on a scouting line.

Q: I can understand your feeling of not wanting to be sort of a sitting duck out there.

Admiral Coye: Well, also, I think it was this patrol or maybe the next one where we did see a submarine on the surface and in distance, and we thought it was one of our own on the scouting line, and it turned out later that it wasn't one of our own. It was one of the Japanese submarines. So that could have been embarrassing too. It could have dove and come over. Because we had to make the scouting line run on the surface so you'd have better visibility. So it wasn't very good.

Q: When you're commanding a submarine, am I gathering that you were always more comfortable submerged than on the surface?

Admiral Coye: Oh, depending. In general, our submarines were designed to run on the surface. They were basically surface cruisers that could dive. On the surface you could make 18 or 20 knots, whereas once you submerged, you were restricted to your battery capacity, and you could either run at two or three knots for 24 hours, or if you ran eight knots you could do that for about an hour, and then if your battery was down, you had to surface to charge your

Coye #1 - 70

battery. So you had a lot more freedom if you were on the surface. As I say, unless you were in sight of enemy territory--land--in the daytime, normally we made our patrols on the surface. I'd say of my time in the patrol area, probably at least 90% was on the surface.

Q: You'd go on the surface until you saw a contact and then dive in order to make your attack?

Admiral Coye: Yes. And of course we had to watch out for planes. But in normal weather conditions, you could see the plane before he could see you, and we could dive within 35 to 40 seconds.

We did have an aircraft radar which never worked very well, and we also had a surface radar which could detect low-flying aircraft. And, of course, undoubtedly some of our 52 submarines that were lost were lost due to aircraft sighting them on the surface. We were fortunate, and we dove many times for aircraft. I don't know the total number in the patrols, but it became more or less routine. If you were chasing a convoy--and some of their planes were big planes, like the four-engine seaplanes, the Mavises--why, we could see them many miles away in clear weather, and they couldn't see us, or didn't see us. We could stay on the surface and watch the plane. They were slow planes, so if they turned toward you, you had plenty of time to dive.

Q: How long did you stay in port before you were assigned on a second patrol? What was the usual turnaround time?

Admiral Coye: The usual turnaround time was about three weeks. You had two weeks in which the crew was sent to a rest camp or recreation area, and then they came back. During that time, the refit crew, which was from the tender, would go through the submarine and make all the repairs that were necessary and load the torpedoes, things like that, get it ready for the next patrol. Then the regular crew would come back, and it would take about a week for them to run some exercises, drills, exercise torpedo firings. Then about a week after that, you'd go back out to sea again.

Q: What did you do in the interval? Were you supervising the entire submarine overhaul?

Admiral Coye: No, they moved us ashore. In Brisbane there, they had an apartment that submarine skippers stayed at. Of course, we'd go down to the office and read the patrol reports of other submarines and just shoot the breeze. I liked to swim, so I went to the beach quite often. In general, we just enjoyed ourselves.

They had a policy that 25% of the crew was changed each time in between, during refit. When you came in, you had to transfer 25% of your crew, and they either went to the refit crew or they went back to new construction. At that time, of course, we had new construction submarines, so they needed experienced personnel, and they would send these men back for commissioning a new submarine.

Q: I'd like to know--because we're talking about the first patrol and of course it will apply, I presume, to all of them--what is your mental attitude when you are out on patrol? Is it a matter of constant tension? I'd just like to have you describe what being on patrol is like.

Admiral Coye: As someone has said (I forget who it was), you're either bored to death or scared to death most of the time. No, of course my own personal attitude was that I should try to remain rested, so in case something came up I would be fresh. So I spent probably more time in my bunk on patrol than anybody else. I did stay rested.

For the crew, they always had a poker game going in the crew's mess. But we didn't let anybody play in the poker game unless they were qualified in submarines. Qualification was similar to the officers' qualification--before they could wear the dolphins, they had to know everything about the submarine. This would take them probably about two patrols, if they were fresh out of submarine school, to get qualified. So those men had to devote their time to their qualification, but the rest of the crew, they read or they played cards.

Later on we had movies, but at this time we didn't have movies. But later on we had movies.

Q: Was it a constant tension or was it a relaxed atmosphere?

Coye #1 - 73

Admiral Coye: We tried to more or less keep it relaxed if we could, because people are more efficient if they're relaxed than under high tension. And of course during attacks or depth charge attacks, evasion, there's bound to be tension. You can't get rid of that very well.

Q: I would think being on the surface would be a much more relaxed atmosphere than being submerged. Is that true or not?

Admiral Coye: No, not necessarily. Submerged, if you're not making an attack or something, is really fairly dull, because you know that no airplane is going to get you, and that's more relaxed to be submerged.

Q: I see.

Admiral Coye: Particularly if there's any heavy seas running, it's calmer too.

Q: Did you have any trouble with people being seasick?

Admiral Coye: Oh, they get over it. They might at first, but they get over it. With any chronic seasickness, they would get transferred.

Coye #1 - 74

Q: Clay Blair says that between June to December of 1943 the best scores were turned in by John Coye on Silversides. So then I think that takes us to the second patrol which left Brisbane in October, I think.

Admiral Coye: Left on the fifth of October.

Q: And what was your area assigned?

Admiral Coye: Let's see. In general, that was again between Rabaul and Truk. That was our area---more or less the same area we'd had before.

Q: I understand you went into Pearl at the end of that patrol.

Admiral Coye: That's correct, because our normal base was Pearl. We were assigned to Squadron Ten, and Squadron Ten was based in Pearl. When we went down to Brisbane, we were only on loan to Brisbane. It wasn't our home squadron, so to speak. But Brisbane had suffered some losses. They had lost about three boats there shortly before that, so we had gone down to be a replacement for one of those boats.

Q: I see.

Admiral Coye: We normally were a Squadron Ten boat, which was based

Coye #1 - 75

in Pearl.

Q: I see. And you were gone, then, according to what you have there, I think 36 days. Is that fair?

Admiral Coye: That's right. That was one of the patrols that we ran out of torpedoes and were able to come back early.

Q: And what did the torpedoes do? Did the torpedoes explode prematurely again on the second patrol?

Admiral Coye: On that patrol, we had two prematures, as I remember it. Yes, we had two prematures on that patrol. We had some hits that time, and we ended up sinking a couple of ships.

Q: Would this be correct that you sank four ships on that second patrol?

Admiral Coye: I think that's correct.

Q: That, I thought, was what Blair was relating to when he said it was the best scores for that period of time.

Admiral Coye: Yes, we sank four ships in that time. One of those I have movies of. One of them was the Jahore Maru, which we had hit, and there's a picture of it right there, the top one. We hit it right amidships, but it didn't sink. So it was left behind, abandoned by the convoy. We came up and tried to sink it with gunfire. I forget how many shots were fired, but we shot quite a few shots at it with our 4-inch gun and that didn't sink it. So we eventually put another torpedo into it which broke its back and it sank. This was a daytime surface attack---which is fairly unusual, that you can make a daytime shot at a ship on the surface.

Q: What type ship was that?

Admiral Coye: It was a transport.

Q: Was it incoming? Was it bringing men in, or had it discharged its load and going back?

Admiral Coye: I forget. I think it was bringing people in, as I recall. Of course, many of those had probably been rescued.

Q: What happened, as I see, is that this would be your first actual sinking. Is that correct?

Admiral Coye: That's right. Well, not this particular ship, but we sank the Tairin Maru, and in the debris we got a life ring from that. We sank the Kazan Maru and got a life ring from that. Somebody said the Americans fought the war for the souvenirs, but we brought back the life rings. And we also got a deck gun from the Tairin Maru; this was about a 30 or 40 millimeter field piece that was to be used by the troops, and it was on the bridge of this ship. The bridge was wooden, and it floated, so we recovered the gun and brought it back to Pearl Harbor where it was turned over to the intelligence people. It was the first one they had seen of that type, as I remember it. Then that gun later is back in New London. It was, for a while, mounted outside the submarine school. I'm not sure where it is now—whether it's in that submarine museum, but that's where it should be. We brought the gun back.

That was a short patrol, and it was a successful patrol.

Q: I'm sure the morale of the crew reflected that.

Admiral Coye: Yes.

Q: Of the four ships, what were the types?

Admiral Coye: Three of them were cargo ships and one of them, the Johore Maru, was a passenger/cargo ship. Out of those four ships sunk in that patrol, three of them were sunk in one attack, or hit in one attack. The Johore was later sunk. The Johore, the Kazan, the Tennan, were all hit with one salvo of torpedoes.

Coye #1 - 78

Q: That's kind of remarkable, isn't it?

Admiral Coye: Yes. After we had expended all our torpedoes, we were then ordered to go back to our home port, which was Honolulu. Also on this patrol we did have a prospective commanding officer, Cy Cole out of the class of '35.[*] He was with us and later got command of his own submarine.

Of course, while we were in Honolulu, on the refit, they put the whole submarine crew up at the Royal Hawaiian Hotel, which had been turned over to the submariners for rest and recreation. As I recall, we paid a dollar a day for room and board there. Everybody enjoyed Honolulu, though some of the crew preferred the refits in Australia. Honolulu was a good place---a lot of beach and swimming and healthful exercise.

Q: And a beautiful hotel.

Admiral Coye: Yes.

Q: So then after your rest and recreation (as they used to call it), you then went on a third patrol. I have information that says you left in December from Pearl.

Admiral Coye: Yes, we left on, I believe it was, the 4th of December

---
[*]Lieutenant Commander Cyrus C. Cole, USN.

from Pearl Harbor. This time we were assigned an area off of Palau. Area Ten was the name of the area.

On the way out to the area, we were directed to spend a day circling Wake Island to see what was going on there. We took pictures of Wake and watched them. I remember seeing cranes working in the lagoon, and we saw the guns they had there. Radars were rotating; at night they had searchlights. There was a cargo ship there on the beach that looked like they might be trying to refloat. But it never did get refloated, as was subsequently shown.

Then we headed for Palau. Palau was a good area. Palau had what were called temperature gradients. A temperature gradient is a difference in the temperature of the seawater. At around 200 feet in Palau, why, the water would normally become markedly colder. This meant that the sound waves would be deflected, so if you could get below the 200 feet and an escort was pinging on you, he wouldn't get any return from the echo. Of course, this change in water temperature didn't protect you from depth charges. Depth charges went right through the gradient, but it was comforting to know that he wasn't able to hold contact on you. That was a good feature of Palau.

Also, it had another good feature in that the one main harbor there had only two entrances—one on the east side and one on the west side. It was a fairly large Japanese base, and the chances were that if you got in close enough to those entrances that you could get a target either going in or coming out. Of course, this meant normally a submerged periscope attack.

Coye #1 - 80

Also around Palau there was a big open sea area, and if you could get contact on a convoy in the open sea, you had time to make a night attack, a night surface attack, which was far more preferable than the periscope attacks. So we were pleased to get assigned to the Palau area.

Q: You had some good contacts on your third patrol.

Admiral Coye: Right. As I say, we were patrolling close in to the harbor entrance, and we noticed that there was a ship that came out of the harbor and hugged the reefs and went into another very small harbor. We determined that it was probably going in there to load bauxite and then would probably return to the main harbor where it would wait until a convoy left. So we watched the ship in this little bauxite loading place, and after I think about two days or so, it came out and headed down the coast of the reef, hugging the reef with an escort, and we fired at that ship. I, at the time, thought we had missed, because we heard the torpedoes hit the reef and explode. We also watched one of the torpedoes smoking badly as it was going toward the ship. That's disappointing, because it means that torpedoes can be sighted easily. At least that particular one was. In any event, I didn't report any damage on that ship, though subsequently, after the war, we were given credit for that ship. It's never shown up in any of the records, but SubPac said that that ship had been sunk, and that we were the only submarine around at the time and it probably belonged to the <u>Silversides</u>.

In any event, after that we had been patrolling in close, so we went out and headed up toward Japan, northwest of Palau. We were fortunate in coming across a convoy headed for Palau. We went in and we attacked. This was at night on the surface. It was early in the morning, around 2:00 o'clock, and we headed in toward the convoy, tracked it and then the convoy zigged right toward us. We ended up being in the middle of the convoy, pretty much. We pulled out and fired torpedoes from our stern tubes, and the ship that we fired at, the column, it missed but it hit the far column of the convoy and sank a ship over there. That attracted the escorts over there, and they started depth charging in the vicinity of the sinking ship and then the convoy became very confused and dispersed, and one ship in the convoy started following us, thinking we were an escort, and we fired a couple of torpedoes at him. The range, I think, was too close and the torpedoes hadn't had time to arm. We missed that, but then later on, we fired some more torpedoes, and we got three ships out of that convoy before it started getting light and then we had to dive.

Q: That was a remarkable experience as well, wasn't it?

Admiral Coye: Yes, very exciting.

Q: What were they carrying? Did you know?

Coye #1 - 82

Admiral Coye: I don't know what they were carrying--probably supplies to Palau. Probably troops and supplies.

Q: By this time it would appear that your torpedoes then were improved.

Admiral Coye: Our torpedoes were running better. By this time, we had inactivated the magnetic exploder and were using contact exploders. But we still managed to get a couple of prematures in that run. No, we didn't have any prematures on that run. We made 11 torpedo hits, as I have it figured here.

Q: You must have expended all your torpedoes by that time?

Admiral Coye: No, we still had a few left. That next day we were in the general area of where the ships had gone down, and there were life boats there and with people in them. We figured that they would send somebody out to rescue the life boats, and they did. A couple of destroyers came by, but by this time we only had torpedoes left in our after tubes. I think we had four left. I was trying to get set up on the destroyers, but they didn't come close enough, and they were very smart. When they spotted the life boats, then they sent out small trawlers that were too small to hit with a torpedo to rescue the people in the life boats. So we only had, I think, four torpedoes left and we went over to the other side of the island, the east coast.

Eventually, we picked up a convoy of two tankers which were headed for Truk. We tried to make an attack on them and the weather was bad, as I remember it, and the torpedoes missed. However, we kept contact with the tankers, and we kept contact with them for just about a week. We followed them for over 1400 miles practically all the way to Truk. We sent out messages homing in other submarines. I remember we got the Muskallunge, which came in and made an approach. I think she might have gotten one hit--I don't remember--but it didn't slow the tankers down too much. We were sounding off a couple of times a day, telling everybody where these tankers were, but we watched them eventually head into Truk. It was very disappointing. Of course, we couldn't make any more attacks, because we had fired all our torpedoes. We were trying to bring other submarines in to make an attack. After that, we headed back to Pearl.

Q: Did any Japanese submarine ever find you?

Admiral Coye: Oh yes. Let me see. I think that was on this patrol. Yes, this was during the daytime. The officer of the deck was Gene Malone.* He spotted torpedoes heading toward us, and he did an abrupt maneuver and avoided the torpedoes. Then we retired; we put the Japanese submarine astern and went full power to get out of the area. I figured as soon as we got over the horizon that I would dive and

---

*Lieutenant (junior grade) Eugene I. Malone, USN.

then reverse course and then come back and try to catch the Japanese submarine when he surfaced. During that time that we had run full power, I think the engineers had gotten a little carried away with the thing and put too much power on the motors and generators, because shortly after we dived, word was passed "fire in the maneuvering room." Of course the maneuvering room is one of the crucial things on the submarine. We're electric drive, so the only connection between the engines and generators and the motors was through the big switchboard in the maneuvering room. If anything happens to that, you have no propulsion, and you're dead in the water. So we dove and it turned out later that the insulation—a submarine is lined with cork insulation to keep moisture down and keep condensation down. The bus bars in the maneuvering room had gotten so hot that they had ignited this cork and had filled the maneuvering room full of smoke. We used all our fire extinguishers trying to put out the fire. We had CO_2 extinguishers, hand-carried ones. We used all those, and people who were fighting the fire had to put on rescue breathing apparatus, and men were starting to pass out. We hadn't been able to put power on the shafts, because we didn't know what the damage was. So I decided that maybe the best thing to do would be to surface and ventilate the boat and check for damage and we had to let the attack on the Japanese submarine go by this time.

Q: When the OOD first saw the periscope, what maneuver did he make?

Admiral Coye: Well, he did what we call try to "comb the track"—that is, to parallel the track to the torpedo so that it would pass one side or the other. One of them did pass about 50 yards on one side and the other about 75 yards on the other. So he was very successful in doing that.

Q: I think the phrase "comb the track" is very interesting and not usual.

Admiral Coye: After the tanker entered Truk and since we were out of torpedoes, ComSubPac ordered us to return to Pearl Harbor. I think actually we came into Midway and then to Pearl Harbor. Anyhow, we returned to Pearl Harbor.

Q: I read a phrase in Roscoe's book and it says, "Lieutenant Commander Coye sweeping the seas between the Marianas and the Carolines with her famous broom."[*] Was that related to your third patrol?

Admiral Coye: Oh, normally when you had fired all of your torpedoes, when you came into port you hoisted a broom and lashed it to the periscope.

---

[*]Theodore Roscoe, United States Submarine Operations in World War II (Annapolis, U.S. Naval Institute, 1949).

Coye #1 - 86

Q: But I was interested. He said the Marianas and the Carolines. Were you in that area on your third patrol?

Admiral Coye: Well, we were more or less in the Carolines.

Q: That's how he's phrasing your third patrol. I think it's interesting and I want to put it on the tape now that you had done a nice job of taking a map of the area and indicating on it your various patrols which I think is interesting and helpful.

Admiral Coye: Well, it's not a very good map; I'll admit to that. But it does clarify a little bit as to when we started and left and the general area in which we went.

Q: I think that's important.

Admiral Coye: But the complete track charts are on file with the original patrol report. I'm not exactly sure where you'd find them.

Q: You told me, I believe, that the patrol reports would be available at Groton, the submarine museum.

Admiral Coye: Yes, the patrol reports are available there. Copies of them are.

Q: And you think the track ...

Admiral Coye: I'm not sure about where the track charts would be, but they ...

Q: They do exist?

Admiral Coye: They do exist. We had to make track charts of each patrol.

Q: I see.

Admiral Coye: I'm sure they must have saved them someplace.

Q: So you came back from your third patrol around the end of the year—didn't you—around the end of 1943? No, I'm mistaken, because you left on your third patrol in December of 1943 and you returned in January of 1944?

Admiral Coye: The 11th of January, 1944.

Q: So having gone back to Pearl early in 1944, you were soon to go on your fourth patrol. Is that correct?

Admiral Coye: That is correct. My fourth patrol, which was the ninth patrol of the <u>Silversides,</u> we were again assigned an area off Palau, although we went by way of Saipan and Guam.

After arriving off Palau, we conducted a close-in patrol of the harbor entrance in Palau, and we sighted some ships exiting the harbor around 9:00 in the morning. We were in very close to the harbor, and there were about three destroyers and two cruisers. They came out of the harbor, and as they cleared the harbor, of course, they speeded up. These were very valuable targets, and we were trying to get a torpedo setup on the cruisers. The destroyer had passed about less than 100 yards from us. I watched him through the periscope. But the cruisers were zigzagging as soon as they left the harbor, and I estimated at one point the closest range was about 2,800 yards. That was as the cruiser was abeam, and he was speeding up, so the torpedo run would have been well in excess of that; it would probably have been closer to 3,500 yards. Since the torpedo data computer didn't have a solution, I didn't fire. Later, thinking it over, I probably should have taken a chance since they were such valuable targets. However, the sea was very calm and glassy and there were lots of float planes around. We were in close to the reef, so we would have been limited in any evasive tactics we could have taken. In any event, we didn't fire, and I regret that we didn't because it would have been worth a shot, even if we had missed. But, as I say, if we had revealed our presence there that close to the reef, we would have had a hard time taking proper evasive procedures, and we might not have made it back.

Q: So you had to make a judgment based on your experience.

Admiral Coye: Yea, I made a judgment and, as I say, the torpedo solution was not checking, because the targets were increasing speed all the time, working probably up to 25 knots or more. They went by awful fast.

Q: How long a time do you have to make a decision? A matter of seconds?

Admiral Coye: Well, no, it's a matter of maybe a minute or so.

Q: And what do you consider a good distance for it?

Admiral Coye: See, a torpedo travels in high speed at 1,500 yards a minute, so it would take a torpedo at over 3,000 yards, it would take the torpedo over two minutes to get there. If they spotted the torpedo, it would give the ships ample time to evade. Normally I tried for torpedo runs of less than 2,000 yards, just a little over a minute for the torpedo to get there. If you get it in too close, then the target is going by too fast, the relative bearing is going by so fast that you're apt to miss it, because it's just going by so fast. It's like driving a car or something like that. You estimate whether you're on a collision course with a target or not. So around 1,000 or 2,000 yards is a good firing range. In night attacks you can usually do a little bit more and take it up to 3,000 yards, because there the target won't see the torpedo and you've solved the course. You have radar and so you've solved the target speed more accurately and you can afford to shoot at a little longer range. There again, at night if you get in too close, things are going to get rushed and odds are the escorts are going to see you and that will throw things off and you'll miss.

Q: Hundreds of factors you must consider before you make a decision.

Admiral Coye: Right.

Q: And you are the man to make it, right?

Admiral Coye: Yes. As I say, I've thought of those cruisers a couple of times since then. I probably should have shot at them, but then I didn't.

Q: The "ifs" in life; you say if you had to do it over again, you probably would have shot at them.

Admiral Coye: Yes, I probably would.

Q: But you're here to tell your story, so maybe you made the right decision.

Coye #1 - 91

Admiral Coye: Let's see. After that, we patrolled around Palau, and we found a convoy on the eastern side of the island. We made an attack and we sank one ship in that convoy. Then we chased that convoy, trying to get ahead of it and make more attacks on it, but as I recall, the escorts were very alert on that convoy and they kept us from getting in any more attacks.

Q: Are their escorts generally destroyers?

Admiral Coye: Destroyers or Chidoris, which are like our PC boats. So we kept reporting the convoy's position and then since the convoy was heading for Rabaul and since we were then getting closer to Brisbane than we were to Pearl Harbor, why, ComSubPac told us to shift control to Brisbane, to Task Force 72. We shifted control and got assigned an area of off New Guinea and went off Manaquore Harbor. There I made an attack on a small freighter that was towing an escort which apparently had been disabled. It was about to approach into the harbor and I fired at it. And I saw the torpedo hit. I thought the ship had sunk, but apparently it didn't because we didn't get credit for it--either that or the ship was not listed in the Japanese postwar periods. But I didn't actually see the ship sink, so I couldn't fight it.

Since we still had a lot of torpedoes left, that was one patrol where I asked for an extension on the time, on the normal 30 days. I received that for another eight or ten days. Then we finally worked

Coye #1 - 92

our way back to Brisbane and arrived there on April eighth. That was my longest patrol. We had been gone...

Q: Would 52 days be correct? It doesn't seem long enough, though. Does 53 days seem like a fair assessment of that patrol?

Admiral Coye: Well, it seemed a lot longer because it was, in a way, a disappointing patrol in that we hadn't sunk many ships. I think we only got two ships in that patrol and we had come back with quite a few torpedoes. But the torpedoes were behaving better. We didn't have any prematures that run.

Q: That was an improvement, at least.

Admiral Coye: That was an improvement, yes.

Q: And then you ended in Brisbane?

Admiral Coye: We ended in Brisbane.

Q: So we're coming up on your fifth patrol now.

Admiral Coye: Right. My fifth, which was the <u>Silversides</u>' tenth. We left Brisbane on the 26th of April. In this patrol I had a new executive officer. My previous one, Bob Worthington, who had done so well and was so good with torpedo data computer had been relieved to go back and get his own boat. Then the fellow who relieved him was Chuck Leigh, out of the class of '39, who had had command of an S-boat.* Instead of staying on the S-boat a little longer and normally waiting to get his own boat, he wanted to get experience in a fleet submarine more in a war zone. He volunteered for the Silversides, and I was extremely happy to get him. He turned out to be a very fine executive officer. He was most aggressive; he had in Academy times been a wrestling champion, and he was very popular with the crew and yet he ruled them with an iron hand. He was an all-around fine officer. He was a good navigator. He could go up and shoot a few stars and get us a position within minutes, whereas Bob Worthington was a good navigator but he was more meticulous. He would shoot at least five stars and take a little longer to work them out. But you could know that you were within a half mile of where he said you were. Anyhow, I was glad to get Chuck Leigh. He was an excellent officer.

So we left Brisbane and headed up along the coast through the Vitiaz Strait and the Admiralty Islands and headed up for an area in the Marianas. Our first part of the patrol was off Guam. Later I was to become more familiar with Guam. We were patrolling off Port Apra in Guam, a submerged patrol, and we sighted a convoy. It was heavily escorted. It had at least five escorts and we made a periscope attack, and we heard one hit. By this time in the stern tubes we were

---

*Lieutenant Charles F. Leigh, USN.

carrying the electric torpedoes, the Mark 18, which supposedly are wakeless, but they don't go as fast as the steam torpedoes. Anyhow, we heard one hit and then were forced deep by the escorts. We got credit for damaging one ship.

The next day we sighted a seven-ship convoy standing out of Port Apra, and it had quite a few escorts. We decided that we would give this convoy a night attack. So we headed down the convoy's track and watched for the convoy smoke and then surfaced as soon as we were out of sight of the convoy, about 5:00 o'clock. We made contact with the convoy that night and tracked it and then we dove for attack just before dawn. We made attacks and fired six torpedoes and we were able to sink three ships out of the convoy with that.

Q: Is that the famous day of May 10?

Admiral Coye: Yes, that's May 10th. We were very heavily depth charged after that attack, because this was a submerged attack and we had two barrages of about 25 depth charges each. I think what had happened was one of the ships we had sunk had been an escort, a gunboat, converted escort, and when it sank, all its depth charges went off at once.

Q: How far were you down?

Admiral Coye: Oh, by this time we were down to our usual evasion depth of around 300 feet.

Q: It still gives you an awful shaking up, doesn't it?

Admiral Coye: Oh yes.

Q: Terrible. Do you want to put in the names of those three ships, Admiral?

Admiral Coye: Yes, if you want. The names of those ships were the Okinawa Maru, Mikage Maru #18 and the Choan Maru #2. The Choan Maru #2 was the gunboat. The Mikage Maru #18 I have a picture of because it didn't sink right away. So one ship, the Mikage Maru, hadn't sunk. We were getting ready in the afternoon to surface and try to sink it by gunfire, but about the time we were getting ready to surface, an airplane started circling it. Of course we were not very far from Guam. While we were getting ready to fire another torpedo into her, why, it sank of its own accord, going down bow first. So we took pictures of that. Next we headed up toward Saipan.

Q: I want to put in the record something that the books speak of of Silversides. Because it says, "John Coye in Silversides entered the Marianas performing like a one-boat wolf pack." He's of course relating to the ones you just talked about and the ones that are upcoming.

Admiral Coye: In the Marianas, Guam, and Saipan, there were quite a few submarines involved in this. We were in what was called, as I recall, "convoy college." By this, the areas were divided up into subareas. You had a schedule in which you rotated your area. For example, you'd spend maybe two days in an area close to a port, Port Apra or Saipan, and then maybe you'd have two days in which you were assigned an area in the outer regions where you could patrol on the surface. There was a regular rotating schedule which we were following at this time. The submarines would rotate every other day or so, so that you didn't have to spend all the time in close in ports submerged or you didn't have to spend all the time out in the outer areas.

Q: I presume the Japanese knew that you were there to keep them from reinforcing the Marianas.

Admiral Coye: Right.

Q: Knowing that we were going to make a landing or an invasion in that area.

Admiral Coye: Right. Yes, the invasion came a month or two later.

Q: So it must have been a very dangerous patrol area because of their knowledge of why you were there?

Coye #1 - 97

Admiral Coye: There were a lot of escorts and a lot of planes there. Our next attack, I recall, was off Guam in which we got two hits and sank Shosei Maru; she was a converted gunboat.

Q: Before you go any further, I don't know what "maru" means. Does that mean "ship"?

Admiral Coye: That means "ship," yes. They're all "marus."

Q: I see that. Thank you.

Admiral Coye: And here again, we made this daytime periscope attack in close to Guam at Apra Harbor. We got there one of the worst depth chargings that I think I had experienced so far. We were evading for four or five hours, as I recall, and had about 61 depth charges. Some of them were fairly close.

Q: Was damage done to your boat?

Admiral Coye: Oh, the usual damage of breaking light bulbs and things like that. But you could tell when a depth charge was close. It's sort of like thunder and lightning. The damage done by a depth charge was when it clicked. The noise was not the damage; the click was transmitted almost instantaneously, whereas the noise went the speed of sound through water. The click was a pressure thing. If the time between the click and the noise was appreciable, that meant that the depth charges weren't too close. But if the click and the noise was simultaneous, then you knew the depth charges were pretty close.

Q: What do you mean by "click"?

Admiral Coye: You could hear it in the hull.

Q: Something hitting the hull?

Admiral Coye: It's the pressure wave hitting the hull.

Q: Just as you say, like thunder and lightning, to estimate the closeness of it.

Admiral Coye: Yes. So it wasn't the noise that you worried about. It was those clicks that you worried about because that's what was doing the damage to the submarine.

So that was one of the severest depth charges we had had. That was right off Guam.

Then we changed areas and went up off Saipan. We sighted a convoy while we were in one of the distant areas off Saipan. In the morning we sighted smoke; we tracked it during the day. Then at night we went in and made an attack and we fired. There were two ships in this convoy. We attacked both the ships simultaneously, and then I've never seen such explosions and flames as I saw there, because the ships must have both been loaded with gasoline. They really lit up the sky.

Q: You got both of them?

Admiral Coye: We got both of them. Yes, simultaneously. Both the ships sank within three minutes.

Q: Oh, my!

Admiral Coye: So they were really hit.

Q: Do you want to put in the names of those two tankers?

Admiral Coye: They were the Shoken Maru and the Horaizan Maru. So by this time we were getting fairly low on torpedoes. I think we only had torpedoes left in the after tubes.

A couple of days later, we sighted a convoy heading into Guam. There were other submarines in the area. I remember one of them was the Shark. We exchanged calls. She was, I think, part of a wolf pack. Then since we were almost out of torpedoes, we agreed that I should go in and make the first attack. I fired four torpedoes with the stern tubes, which were the electric torpedoes. They missed. So I turned the convoy over to the Shark and then we headed home, because we were all out of torpedoes and we headed back to Pearl Harbor. Later the same day we sighted smoke at another convoy which we tracked and sent a contact report to ComSubPac. Wish we had had more torpedoes.

Q: You must have felt that that patrol was quite successful.

Admiral Coye: Yes, we had. We had gotten 12 hits with that patrol and hadn't had any prematures. I think we had sunk a total of six ships in that patrol.

Q: That was when they said you were a one-man wolf pack, or a one-boat wolf pack.

Admiral Coye: It was an excellent patrol. So we arrived in Pearl Harbor on the 11th of June. The Silversides at this time had made ten patrols and was due for a navy yard overhaul. So we were sent back to Mare Island Navy Yard for overhaul. This was a welcome change. Betty and most of the other wives came out to the West Coast, and it was a very enjoyable period.

Q: How long did that take, the overhaul?

Admiral Coye: We arrived in Mare Island on the 19th of June, and we left for Pearl Harbor on the 4th of September.

Q: Just three months.

Admiral Coye: Not quite three months.

Q: They gave the ship three months rest and recreation, right?

Admiral Coye: Yes. There they did some alterations on us. We had a 40-millimeter gun that we had sort of stolen. Well, not stolen but we had gotten cumshaw down in Australia and they moved that from on deck up to what we called the cigarette deck, which is just aft of the bridge. We were one of the first submarines to get this 40-millimeter gun. I got it in that last refit down in Australia. The Army had these guns, and I got to know some of the Army officers and I gave one of them a bottle of whiskey, and he gave me a gun.

Q: A fair trade?

Admiral Coye: So we had that permanently installed on the cigarette deck. It wasn't designed to be a waterproof gun, but if you kept it greased well, the firing mechanism would work and it was what we thought of as a good addition to the ship. Oh, there are numerous other alterations that they found necessary.

Q: Did you hate to go back or were you anxious to go back? Or did you just figure this is the way the job goes?

Coye #1 - 102

Admiral Coye: Well, I enjoyed the time with the family, but I realized I didn't have much choice. Yes, I was glad to get back underway again.

Q: How many children did you have by this time?

Admiral Coye: By this time I had two.

Q: A boy and ...

Admiral Coye: And a girl.

Q: His name is John?

Admiral Coye: John, yes.

Q: And the girl is ...

Admiral Coye: That's Beth.

Q: We're going to talk about Beth a little later.

Admiral Coye: Yes. But the children stayed on the East Coast. But Betty had spent the war in Stockbridge, Massachusetts, where her sister lived.

Q: How long did it take you to go from San Francisco back to Pearl Harbor?

Admiral Coye: Oh, that was a fast trip, I think. Three of us went back together--the *Trigger*, the *Salmon*, and the *Silversides*. So we stuck together. One interesting thing was that we made sort of a race out of it. Since the *Trigger* was a sister ship of the *Silversides*, it had the same engines and everything. We challenged them to a race and the *Salmon* was a different class, so she was to be the umpire. This was on the way to Pearl. The *Silversides* and *Trigger* submerged and then the *Salmon* fired a flare, and we both did what we call a "battle surface," going full power and ran full power for an hour and whoever was ahead was the winner. Of course, the crew got word of this, and we worked up some money bets. As I remember, it was over $500 we had on this race. Unfortunately, the story doesn't end well, because the *Trigger* beat us, but she had--not really cheated, but while we were running full power on the surface, she had blown out all her extra variable ballast to make herself lighter. She couldn't have dived at the end of the race. But we kept our variable ballast and could have dived. In any event, she didn't beat us by much, but she did a little bit.

Q: Well, that's kind of cheating, isn't it?

Admiral Coye: Yes. And, as I remember, the ships were designed for around 19 knots and in our log it showed we were making 21 knots during that race. Of course, we both had clean bottoms and had the overloads tied down and everything. It was a lot of fun, but cost us a little money. <u>Trigger</u> and <u>Silversides</u> were always very competitive with each other. At that time the <u>Trigger</u>'s skipper was Fritz Harlfinger.* I don't know whether you know him or not.

Q: I know the name.

Admiral Coye: We always had a lot going on between us. Our patrols usually coincided, too.

Q: But on your other patrols, I'd just like to say this right now that you were up to this point a single submarine going out to your area. Later the wolf packs ...

Admiral Coye: The wolf packs came. Yes, of course by this time we had captured Saipan and Guam and pretty soon, I think, Palau. The submarine areas were no more there, so the total area for submarines was becoming less and less. We were getting new boats out; we were getting more and more submarines, so you had to put them in wolf packs. They could no longer afford to give one area and say, "This is your area." You had to put them in wolf packs.

---

*Lieutenant Commander Frederick J. Harlfinger II, USN, who eventually became a vice admiral.

Coye #1 - 105

Q: I sort of thought the wolf pack was an idea of Lockwood's, of, "Let's do it this way." But you're saying it was sort of, you couldn't help yourself.

Admiral Coye: No, forced into it, more or less. Of course the origin of the wolf packs was the German submarines. The Germans had wolf packs earlier in the war.

When the first wolf packs went out, they would put a division commander in, a senior submarine officer, who was no longer in command of a submarine and he had a division of submarines. So they thought, "Well, we'll put a division commander out there in one of the submarines and he'll be the wolf pack commander." Well, the submarines really only have one periscope to look through when you're making an attack, and the skipper's got to be at that. The division commander can't very well be at it, so it didn't work out too well. In some cases, there wasn't bad blood, but there was arguing between the skipper and the division commander. So they decided to put the senior skipper in charge of the wolf pack, and that worked out much better.

Q: Now, am I getting ahead of your story? Because we are just now back in Pearl after your overhaul.

Admiral Coye: A little bit. On the next patrol we went out as a wolf pack.

Q: Oh, you did go out on number six patrol?

Admiral Coye: Yes, as a wolf pack. I was the senior skipper, so I got to be the wolf pack commander.*

Q: Oh, I didn't know that. That's nice. Did you like that?

Admiral Coye: Well, it has its advantages and disadvantages. In general, I didn't like it as much because you are not only concerned about the safety and whatnot of your own submarine, but you had the problems of the other submarines that were with you.

Q: How many would have been in a wolf pack?

Admiral Coye: In this one there was three. We had the _Trigger_ and the _Salmon_.

Q: The same you had gone out with.

Admiral Coye: Yes. As I say, we all got along fine together, but I personally would have just as soon gone out on my own without having the responsibility of the two other submarines.

---

*This wolf pack was known as "Coye's Coyotes."

Coye #1 - 107

Q: You had to have constant communication, I would expect. Or was that possible?

Admiral Coye: Well, that was one of the problems. We didn't have too good a communication in those days. We could communicate by our radars. We could flash them on and off. We could Morse Code the radars, and that was one method of communicating. Then we had radios, but they didn't always work, very high frequency radios. They supposedly didn't go any long distance but would be good between the submarines. Of course you had to be on the surface to use those. Communications was a bit of a problem. Occasionally we'd come alongside each other and just talk by megaphone.

Q: I was wondering if you would do that. Like having a morning conference.

Admiral Coye: Yes. And by this time we had movies on board. They only had about three or four films that they took out, so we'd go alongside, and somebody in a rubber boat or something would go over and swap movies back and forth.

Q: I think I'm going to interrupt now. Do you want to put in the dates of this patrol?

Admiral Coye: Yes. We left Pearl Harbor for our 11th patrol (which was my sixth patrol) on the 24th of September, and we headed for an area off Formosa. We left together, and we patrolled off Formosa and we didn't have any luck there. I think, as I remember, the _Trigger_ did sight a cruiser, but it couldn't get in close enough to make an attack.

Of course the big event here was when they had the battle off Leyte Gulf there. As soon as we heard about that, we started heading down south toward the area, but as I recall, there was a line of which U.S. submarines were not supposed to go south of from around 18 degrees latitude or somewhere in there. Anyway, we were trying to contact the retiring Japanese fleet, which had been damaged. The _Trigger_ did sight two of the battleships at a distance, and we couldn't get in to make an attack. So then we chased them. They were heading for Japan and we chased them, trying to follow the oil slicks, because they were leaking oil. Even though they were damaged, they were probably making around 20 knots. Then there was a tanker which was to fuel them, and we finally picked up this tanker. I went in and made an attack.

Coye #2 - 109

Interview Number 2 with Rear Admiral John Starr Coye, Jr.,
U.S. Navy (Retired)

Place: Admiral Coye's residence in Coronado, California

Date: 16 September 1982

Subject: Biography

Interviewer: Commander Etta-Belle Kitchen, U.S. Navy (Retired)

Q: We were about at the end of your sixth patrol and the Silversides' 11th patrol when we finished the other tape.

Admiral Coye: We had been trying to track down the Japanese fleet that was heading north, and they had a tanker that was to refuel them. We did make contact with the tanker. So on the 30th of October, just after dawn, the Silversides dove and made an attack on the tanker. Here again, the torpedoes plagued us. By this time, we were shooting electric torpedoes, and their only advantage is that they're wakeless. But in any event, we had obtained good position and fired six torpedoes at the tanker, but unfortunately one of the electric torpedoes apparently didn't run, and as soon as it left the tube it started going down. All torpedoes, when they reach a certain depth, will self-destruct. So this torpedo with its warhead blew up practically right underneath the Silversides--closer, really, than any depth charge we had ever had. Aside from really shaking us up, it alerted the tanker (because this was daytime) and the tanker zigged and was able to avoid the other five torpedoes. That was a very unfortunate experience.

Q: And all due to the fault of the torpedo.

Admiral Coye: All due to the fault of the torpedo. So we sent out contact reports to the Salmon and the Trigger. By this time there was another wolf pack in the area, and we sent it to them too.

So then the next attack was made by the Trigger, and her attack was successful. It slowed the tanker down and stopped it, and it took a big angle, but it didn't sink at that time. So then it was the Salmon's turn, and he went in and he made an attack. He got at least two hits in it, but of course by this time the Japanese had a lot of escorts around trying to protect this damaged tanker. The escorts gave the Salmon a real severe depth charge attack. It turned out that while it had not ruptured the Salmon's hull, it had pushed it in, and the Salmon was forced to surface to keep from going down and being crushed at a depth, so the Salmon surfaced. By this time it was dark, and the Salmon was trying to evade on the surface. First it was successful, but then the escorts saw her, and there was a gun battle between the Salmon and the escorts. The Salmon scored quite a few hits on the escorts, but eventually the Salmon was able to escape more or less into a rain squall. We could see some of this through the periscope. It was a fairly confusing situation, because there were a lot of escorts and, as I say, there were probably four or five submarines all involved. It was hard to tell who was who. We surfaced, trying to draw the escorts away from the _Salmon_, and then one of the escorts started shooting at us. He was getting on fairly close with his gunfire, so we were forced to dive. We eventually shook that escort and surfaced and were glad when we got on the surface to hear the _Salmon_ on the radio. We had made a rendezvous with the _Salmon_ and _Trigger_. By this time the _Sterlet_ was in on the act. She had actually fired at the tanker too. But it was, as I recall, a confusing situation. But we did rendezvous with the _Salmon_, and we got the orders to proceed to Saipan and to escort the _Salmon_. The _Salmon_ was unable to dive, so we formed up in a formation. I had made a decision (we were mainly worried about airplane attacks) that if an airplane came, we would all stay on the surface and try to fight it out with the airplane. Fortunately, no Japanese airplanes found us, though eventually within a day or two we received air coverage from Saipan. They stayed with us all during the day. They said that they had shot down Japanese planes that were trying to get at us. They shot down at least one plane that had been after us.

Q: That was another time in which your luck held.

Admiral Coye: Yes. The _Trigger_ said that she'd been fired at by torpedoes, and actually we sighted torpedo wakes that same night there and avoided those.

Q: When you were escorting her, how far apart would you be?

Admiral Coye: Oh, maybe 1,000 yards or so.

Q: Close.

Admiral Coye: Close, yes, within easy visual range--in loose formation. So we eventually got back to Saipan on the third of November.

Q: Then you went on to Pearl?

Admiral Coye: No, we stayed at Saipan.

Q: And that was considered the end of that patrol?

Admiral Coye: Not really. It was sort of an interlude in the patrol. Then they organized us into a gunnery wolf pack called "Burt's Brooms."

Q: I know the name.

Admiral Coye: This was an idea. The carriers were getting ready to make an attack on Japan. They didn't want to be detected by trawlers or patrol boats while they were running in to make their attack, so somebody had the idea of sending some submarines up there on a sweep and let them clear out all the trawlers. So they organized that. We had six submarines that were organized. Since there were so many submarines, they put a division commander in charge. That was Burt Klakring.* That's why they call it Burt's Brooms.

We left Saipan on the 10th of November and we were going to head up toward the empire. He put us in sort of a formation on a line about 20 miles apart. We were to steam along there. Any patrol boats we saw or trawlers, we were to sink them. This really didn't work out too well. In the first place, it was rather rough weather, so it wasn't good for gun shooting. In the second place, the targets were too small to hit by torpedoes in general.

I can remember we had one gun engagement in which the theory was that if one sighted one, then the fellow next to you would come along and help you out. Well, we and the Trigger got one, and we fired several hundred rounds at this fellow. He was, of course, fairly well armed. The advantages were really all with the trawlers, because one hit in a submarine and you're not longer a submarine if they hole your pressure hull. But we did hit him numerous times and had him on fire, and then the splashes from succeeding shots put the fire out. I think he ended up getting away scot-free, though I'm sure he had a lot of damage. The other boats didn't have too much success either. There were several patrol boats sunk by the other submarines, but in the

---
*Commander Thomas Burton Klakring, USN.

long run they finally cancelled this when they found out there were more patrol boats in the area than there were when they started. So I think they did this one more time, but then they ran the carriers up offside. They figured the submarines would draw the patrol boats away, and the carriers could run up offside. Actually, in this case, the carrier strike was cancelled, so we were just doing this as a dummy run.

Q: An exercise?

Admiral Coye: Yes. They had scheduled this, and they thought they'd see how it goes. But submarines were really not designed for that kind of action.

Q: What submarine did Klakring ride?

Admiral Coye: He rode the <u>Silversides</u>. I had him with me. Oh, we've always been good friends. He was a very successful submarine skipper. He was skipper of the <u>Guardfish</u> during the war. He moved here to Coronado, and we saw quite a bit of him. Unfortunately, he died about two years ago.

Q: What did he think of the exercise?

Admiral Coye: Probably the same thing.

Q: The same thing?

Admiral Coye: Yes.

Q: He got at least fame by being called Burt's Brooms.

Admiral Coye: Yes, and there were some damage done through it. I don't have the patrol reports or the whole summary of Burt's Brooms, but it was, I'd say, partially successful but not an outstanding success.

Recently (May 1983) I had a chance to talk to my classmate, Captain J.F. Enright, who was skipper of Archerfish when it sank the Shinano, the largest Japanese carrier which was on its builders trials on November 19, 1944. He has written an article "The Doolittle Raiders Did More Than Bomb Tokyo" (Copyright 1983) which mentions Burt's Brooms. It appears from Captain Enright's research that the captain of Shinano was influenced in his course decisions by the possibility that there were many more submarines in the area--as there had been when Burt's Brooms were sweeping the seas a little earlier. Thus, if Burt's Brooms did in fact contribute to the sinking of the Shinano, the operation was more successful than was thought at the time.*

---

*This paragraph was inserted by Admiral Coye while reviewing the transcript of the interview.

Coye #2 - 116

After that, they called that off. We were sent to Midway. We arrived in Midway on the 23rd of November 1944 for a refit.

Q: Could we go back to Leyte Gulf? Those Japanese ships which the three of you intercepted---I have a note that you went on the surface in broad daylight with land in view practically?

Admiral Coye: Yes. These were important targets, and we figured the worst they could do was send out a plane at us and then we'd dive. But until they did that, why, we stayed on the surface. We were chasing battleships, and battleships were important targets.

Q: They were the ones that had been damaged at Leyte Gulf?

Admiral Coye: Right.

Q: So now we're back at the Marianas at the end of that patrol, right?

Admiral Coye: No, we came back to Midway. Beautiful Midway.

Q: Beautiful Midway.

Admiral Coye: There's a song written about it---"Beautiful, beautiful Midway."

Q: I don't know that song.

Admiral Coye: There we got a refit, and that was when I was relieved by John Nichols.*

Q: That was the end of your submarine...?

Admiral Coye: That was the end of my patrols.

Q: I read that 11 patrols--that meant 11 for the Silversides.

Admiral Coye: Right. Eleven for the Silversides and six for myself.

Q: And you actually did six of those. Because early the following year, the Silversides did sink more Japanese ships, I believe. But that was after you were detached.

Admiral Coye: There's one more according to this.

Q: I see. One more after you were detached.

Admiral Coye: Right.

Q: Well, we will take a little break now. That ends a very important

---
*Commander John C. Nichols, USN.

Coye #2 - 118

part of your career, don't you consider that?

Admiral Coye: Yes, that was really the highlight of my career, the patrols on the _Silversides_. That's what I figure I was trained for and what I did as well as I could.

Q: Well, there are many citations. There's a citation for your ship and many awards for you. I'm going to just list those awards, and then I will add them at the end of the interview, because the ship itself received a Presidential Unit Citation. Then you received personally the Navy Cross, two gold stars in lieu of the second and third Navy Cross, the Bronze Star Medal, and the Legion of Merit with Combat V authorized for the last two medals. These citations will all be appended to the end of the interview.

Now, we had ended one dramatic period of your Navy life and come to completely different types of assignments, the first one being in New London as the instructor for the prospective commanding officer course. You were there two years, I believe. I wanted you to describe for me your emotions at having such an abrupt change of assignment and way of living and everything, a completely abrupt change.

Admiral Coye: Well, I really didn't feel it was too abrupt, aside from the fact that I was leaving the war zone, so to speak. I was still in a submarine job, and it was an important submarine job in that I was in charge of the PCO school, the prospective commanding officer school at the submarine school in New London. There I was, as I say, still amongst submariners, and I felt I had a very important job in giving to the students, who were all really experienced submarine officers, but training them to be commanding officers and passing along what words of wisdom I could. I enjoyed that tour very much.

By this time, the course was a four-week course that they went through, of which two of the four weeks were spent at sea. So I really still had saltwater in my veins there more or less, so to speak, by going to sea with them and taking the students to sea.

In the school itself, we had two instructors. I was the senior one, and the other instructor was Reuben Whitaker, who had been skipper of the Flasher.* Reuben was, of course, a very successful submarine skipper. Reuben and I were good friends, and it worked out well. I was glad to be back in New London.

When I left Silversides, my wife had been in Stockbridge, Massachusetts, and I went there. We packed up the house and moved down to New London. It was in the middle of winter, wasn't it?

Q: It would have been in March. It was still cold.

Admiral Coye: It was still cold. We found a place to live in New

---
*Commander Reuben T. Whitaker, USN.

Coye #2 - 120

London. We had lived there before, of course, when I went to submarine school, when I was out on the R-boat. So we had a lot of friends and I was glad to be there. The head of the submarine school at the time was Freddie Warder, who was known as "Fearless Freddie" of the Seawolf fame.* So it was a very good atmosphere.

Q: How long did you say the course was?

Admiral Coye: The course itself was four weeks, of which two were spent in the classroom and two were spent at sea.

Q: Is that enough, four weeks?

Admiral Coye: Well, these were all experienced submarine officers, and it was mainly to give them practice in firing torpedoes. That was the basic thing. Then, of course, we gave them courses in evading depth charge attacks, things like that. We gave them courses in that.

Q: It was the same course you had taken.

Admiral Coye: It was the same course I had taken.

Q: Some time before. I'm asking the same questions on it.

---

*Captain Frederick B. Warder, USN.

Admiral Coye: Yes. Except this time, instead of being a student, I was the instructor.

Q: And you told me that when you were a student there were maybe half a dozen of you. Was that still true now?

Admiral Coye: That was still true, because we still kept about six in each class. It varied, but five to seven, I'd say. We still kept the same number, because that way you could organize a torpedo fire control party and allocate the duties amongst them. Anymore than that would have been inconvenient, and with any less we wouldn't have had enough to really organize the fire control party.

Q: We haven't talked about when you went from lieutenant commander to commander.

Admiral Coye: Oh, I forget when that was.

Q: Were you lieutenant commander all during the time you were on submarines, on the Silversides?

Admiral Coye: No, I think I made commander on the Silversides. Yes, I'm pretty sure I did.

Q: And do you remember when you made captain? That's a big step.

Coye #2 - 122

Admiral Coye: Oh, that was quite a bit later. That was in 1949 or 1950, I think.

Q: But you received a letter of commendation for your work there.

Admiral Coye: Yes. We did work hard there and, of course, at the first part the war was still on. It was hard work, good work.

The submarine school is still doing a fabulous job. I went back there recently to see how things were last year, and the present submarine school skipper is a good friend of mine, and he showed me all through the school again. They are still doing a fine job back there in New London.

Q: I thought the commendation with authorization to wear the commendation ribbon from the Commander in Chief U.S. Atlantic Fleet should be quoted. I'm going to read it. It's only three lines, and I think I'd like to put it on the record. It says, "For meritorious conduct while serving as a senior administration instructor of the command class course of the submarine school, U.S. Submarine Base, New London, Connecticut, from January 1945 to September 1945." So that was nice.

Admiral Coye: Yes.

Q: Was that a big ceremony when you received that?

Coye #2 - 123

Admiral Coye: Oh no, I don't remember that it was at all.

Q: Now, let's see. Do we want to talk about any more things there?

Admiral Coye: No, I don't think so. I think that pretty well covered it, the PCO school. After that, I was transferred out to Pearl Harbor again.

Q: You became operations officer on the staff of Commander Submarine Squadron One and that, according to my information, was from March 1947 through June 1948. And was that in Pearl?

Admiral Coye: Yes, that was in Pearl. But I also had an additional duty there, which was to establish a PCO school out in Pearl. Up until this time they hadn't had one. That was really my primary job in going out there, to set up and establish a course at Pearl Harbor, a PCO course. I remember the chief of staff there at that time was Frank Watkins.* He was the one who urged me to take that job, to come out there and set up the school. I did the Squadron One operations job, which was not too involved, so I could do both jobs. I did two jobs out there.

Q: And the war was over by then, of course.

---

*Captain Frank T. Watkins, USN, chief of staff to ComSubPac.

Admiral Coye: The war was over by then, yes.

Q: What did it mean---operations? What did you actually do? I know you set up the school.

Admiral Coye: Oh, that was mainly scheduling the exercises for the submarines and just basically setting the schedule for them, assigning them various duties, exercises to be conducted, torpedo approaches to be conducted. That was basically it.

Q: How large an area did you have?

Admiral Coye: Oh, it was the area around Pearl Harbor; we had a training area there. There was a submarine area, and we were responsible for assigning what ships could go through those areas and what the submarines would do. We ran some convoy exercises. Ships that would be coming into Pearl Harbor, why, we'd intercept them and make believe we were shooting at them and things like that.

Q: How many submarines were you talking about?

Admiral Coye: Oh, the squadron, I think, had about 12 submarines in it, as I remember it.

Q: It seems to me that was just for about a period of a year.

Admiral Coye: Yes.

Q: And then you went on to be commander of Submarine Division 52.

Admiral Coye: Right. Then I had a division. I think we had, as I remember it, six submarines in the division. I used to go on board the various submarines, and when they were going out for exercises, I'd see how they did on their torpedo approaches. There again, we had sort of minor fleet problems.

I remember one time we made a trip to the West Coast, and we were up the Northwest, basically. A division commander just ...

Q: Did you ride all the submarines?

Admiral Coye: Yes, I rode them all at different times. I also had an office ashore at the submarine base there, too. I spent most of my time riding submarines.

Q: Was your family with you?

Admiral Coye: Yes, my family was at Pearl Harbor. We lived there.

Q: And that gave you a two-year period out there.

Admiral Coye: Yes, the first year we lived in a Quonset hut,

Coye #2 - 126

because housing was very short out there. Then we did finally get some Navy housing that was adequate.

The first time we lived in Honolulu we lived on a civilian economy and lived up in Pacific Heights. That was really more interesting, because you got to know the people better. But this time we lived at the naval base.

Q: And then the last part of that year you went to the Armed Forces Staff College?

Admiral Coye: Right. That was, of course, in Norfolk. I was in the sixth class to be graduated from the Staff College. I enjoyed that very much, because it was an opportunity to meet and mingle with the other services. As you know, the students were equally divided among the Army, Navy, and the Air Force. We all shared offices, and we lived in apartments on the base there. They did their best to mix everybody up amongst the Army, Navy, and Air Force. I made some good friends there that have lasted a lifetime in the other services.

It was basically in learning how to write operations orders for joint operations. That was the main subject of the course. We had some very distinguished speakers that came and gave us lectures. It was an interesting course and was well worth attending.

That was just a year or two after we had had this unification of the services.

Q: I was going to ask if that was the result of the unification.

Admiral Coye: The Armed Forces Staff College was a result of the unification. It unified the more or less younger officers, because all the officers were either commanders or majors or lieutenant colonels.

Q: And so then we get up to the year of 1950 and you had a two-year tour on the staff of Commander Operational Development Force in Norfolk.

Admiral Coye: Yes, that was an interesting tour of duty in that the Operational Development Force is responsible for testing new weapons, and my job on the staff of the Operational Development Force was antisubmarine warfare officer. I think they figured it took a thief to catch a thief, so that's why I was given that job, as how to best fight submarines. We had a lot of new developments going. Our main areas where they were tested were down in Key West. That's where the sound conditions are better and where we had ships assigned to the Operational Development Force. They would install these new weapons and new sonar gear and things like that on these ships, and then they'd write up long detailed reports. The idea of the Operational Development Force was to give weapons a test before they were bought in any number. It was a consumer research type of ...

Q: Quality control?

Admiral Coye: Quality control. There was always pressure to quickly say whether these weapons or sonar gear were improved or not or should be bought. We also had the aviation part of antisubmarine warfare too. We had VX-1, which was an experimental squadron. That was also down in Key West. So I spent a lot of time going back and forth from Norfolk to Key West where my project officers were. A lot of the things didn't turn out, but many of them did, and they're in the fleet now. It was interesting to see something develop from an idea to something that was worthwhile.

Q: Did you find problems? Were you able to stop some of the horrible ideas that someone came up with that wouldn't work?

Admiral Coye: Yes, we gave them all a fair test, and if they passed the test, okay. If they didn't, why, they were shelved. One of the interesting projects I had there was that the British had developed in World War II a small submarine called the X-craft. I don't know whether you've ever read about those or not.

They are a four-man submarine that they could put a diver in and he could lock out of the submarine and attach a limpet mine to a ship that was anchored. Then he'd get back in the submarine, and the submarine would theoretically get clear, and the mine would explode and sink the ship. The British were anxious to sell the United States some of these midget submarines. So I was assigned as the project officer for that job. That was most interesting, I got to know some of the British officers who had been involved, during the war, with this X-craft. We made penetrations of nets and things like that, sending a man out with a cutter to cut it underwater. It was a very interesting assignment.

Q: Was it worthwhile?

Admiral Coye: No, we decided that this was not the type of weapon that the United States was really interested in. The Italians had the same ideas with divers attacking ships. But it's really for a nation that doesn't have much to be able to maybe sink a big ship. So it really didn't fall in line with the U.S. philosophy, so we didn't buy any.

Q: And that was your decision? You were the project officer that made that recommendation?

Admiral Coye: Yes.

Q: And they took your recommendation?

Admiral Coye: Yes.

Q: Well, I think that's interesting. Do you remember any of the other developmental craft?

Admiral Coye: Oh, we had the early models of the towed sonar, which is now being used. I remember we had a lot of experiments with that.

We had a lot of experiments with sonar from helicopters, and that is now, of course, being used. There were a lot of projects.

Q: But they all related to submarines?

Admiral Coye: The ones I was involved with, yes.

Q: The Korean War started in that time. Did that affect this job or any of the assignments you had then?

Admiral Coye: No, that didn't affect any of my assignments there at OpDevFor, because there was very little antisubmarine activity in the Korean War.

Q: But you were at Norfolk during that time.

Admiral Coye: Right. My boss was Admiral Curts, "Germany" Curts.[*] He had had a lot to do with developing radar in the first part of

---

[*] Rear Admiral Maurice E. Curts, USN.

World War II. He was a marvelous man.

Q: In any case, every time you went on you were learning more.

Admiral Coye: Right.

Q: Were you aware of that, or did you think, "Oh, this is old hat. I know all that."

Admiral Coye: No. Well, when I left the Staff College I did have an offer of a job up in BuPers writing TAD orders. Well, that really didn't sound very exciting to me, so I turned that down. I had this officer for this other job in OpDevFor and I think I did the right thing.

Q: I should have thought that between the two, this was much more interesting. And then you went, as I understand, to be commanding officer of a sub tender?

Admiral Coye: Yes. When was that? Do you have the date there?

Q: I just have that that was between February of 1952 and September 1953. So that would have been about a year and six months.

Admiral Coye: Right. Well, by this time I had just put on my four

Coye #2 - 132

stripes. So I was due to leave OpDevFor, and the submarine people wanted me back in submarines. So they had this tender available, the Fulton, which was a good tender. Of course, it had been one of the tenders down in Brisbane during the war, but now it was stationed in New London, and I jumped at the opportunity to take command of the Fulton.

The Fulton, of course did refits on submarines, repairs on them. But also in New London, they had a submarine base that did repairs, and so this meant that the Fulton could leave New London and turn over the submarines that it normally would refit to the base. So we got a little bit more sea duty than the normal tender did. The normal tender is so busy tending either submarines or destroyers, and it doesn't get to sea very much. But the Fulton did. For this, I was very glad. I was skipper on there, I think, for 18 months.

First, we went through a navy yard overhaul in Philadelphia and then we went down to Guantanamo for a refresher training. That was interesting. Then we went up to Argentia and made a cruise up there. Then on the East Coast you have the hurricanes come through every now and then, so every time there would be a hurricane watch, I'd call up SubLant and say, "The Fulton shouldn't be alongside the pier during a hurricane; we've got to get to sea." So we'd go to sea. We got a little more sea duty that way, riding out the hurricanes.

So that 18 months on there was very enjoyable. We had plenty of people, as I remember it. We had a crew of around 1,200, so we were able to not only service all the submarines but we were able to keep the ship in number one condition. It was a good ship.

Q: How many submarines could you handle at one time?

Admiral Coye: One squadron was based on us, and that would be about 10 or 12 submarines. Another time we went to sea on the _Fulton_ was when we went down to the Virgin Islands at St. Thomas for an operation that they called Springboard, which they do in the wintertime. The submarines and destroyers go down to good weather. We were based in St. Thomas and more or less acted as the host ship for all the submarines operating out of St. Thomas. That was also a very interesting duty.

Q: I know a tender repairs and services submarines, but how many could you handle at one time? One?

Admiral Coye: No, no. You could handle really as many as you could have alongside, but normally there would only be maybe four or five, possibly six alongside at one time.

Q: That's quite a lot.

Admiral Coye: Yes.

Q: And what happened to their crews? Did they come aboard while you were ...

Admiral Coye: No, they lived on board the submarines.

Q: Oh, they lived in the submarines.

Admiral Coye: But we sent our repair people aboard them to do the repairs.

Q: And that is, the crew would live there but your people would go on and do repairs?

Admiral Coye: Right.

Q: Would the crew help with the repair?

Admiral Coye: In some cases, yes. In some cases, no.

Q: Depending on what the repairs were.

Admiral Coye: Depending on what the repair was, how major it was.

Q: They're enormous ships, the submarine tenders.

Admiral Coye: Yes, they are. And I think the Fulton, if I'm not

Coye #2 - 135

mistaken, is still in commission and it's probably one of the oldest ships in commission, because the <u>Sperry</u>, which was the sister ship, was decommissioned here on the West Coast a few months ago. At that time, it was claimant the record of being the oldest ship. So I think maybe now the <u>Fulton</u> may be the oldest ship in commission.

Q: Of all ships, the oldest ship, period?

Admiral Coye: The oldest ship, period.

Q: It would seem to me it's almost as big as an aircraft carrier.

Admiral Coye: No, it's not anywhere near that.

Q: No, I know it isn't. But I look at them and they just look so big to me.

Admiral Coye: Yes.

Q: But you enjoyed that duty?

Admiral Coye: Yes.

Q: And then you went to command of Submarine Squadron Eight.

Admiral Coye: Right.

Q: So you've been continuing along still with your submarine duties in various aspects of it.

Admiral Coye: Yes. Submarine Squadron Eight was based in New London at the submarine base. The submarine squadron is sort of two divisions, so I had, I think, 12 submarines. Our major event, as I remember, was that we had a big exercise up off of Iceland, which I ran. At that time, since the Fulton was free to leave the base, she left, and I rode the Fulton as the squadron commander. We were trying to see if airplanes and submarines could detect submarines that were trying to come through that gap up there near Iceland. That was an interesting exercise. Lousy weather, but it was a good exercise.

Q: You were there for practically a year on that tour.

Admiral Coye: Yes, about a year.

Q: You rode the Fulton up to this exercise.

Admiral Coye: I rode the Fulton.

Q: Other than that, were you ashore?

Coye #2 - 137

Admiral Coye: Other than that I was ashore. And I would ride the submarines occasionally to see how they were doing on their torpedo firings or for inspections and things like that. A squadron commander is more of an administrator, really, than anything else.

Q: You say you had two divisions?

Admiral Coye: Two divisions there, yes.

Q: And then you stayed right where you were to go to Naval War College?

Admiral Coye: No, that's up in Newport.

Q: Oh, this was in New London.

Admiral Coye: Yes.

Q: And then you went to Newport.

Admiral Coye: Yes. I had a year up there at the Naval War College in the senior command course. I enjoyed that year very much. Of course we had some very good lectures, and then I enjoyed the opportunity of their library. They had a fabulous library. The superintendent was

Lynde McCormick at that time.*

The other accomplishment I had was that some of us got together and built ten boats.

Q: You're making a joke.

Admiral Coye: No, in the hobby shop up there.

Q: How big a boat?

Admiral Coye: Oh, they were little Penguin 11-foot dinghies.

Q: I see. They weren't submarines.

Admiral Coye: No. We had Saturdays free, and on Saturdays we'd go over there and we built ten hulls and then we drew lots for them. So when you were working on them, you didn't know whether that was going to be yours or not, so you were very careful not to mar it or scratch it up. You made a good hull. That was a lot of fun.

Q: What was your main thesis? Or what did you contribute? What did you have to write when you were at the Naval War College?

Admiral Coye: Well, let's see. I wrote a term paper. I think the

---
*Vice Admiral Lynde D. McCormick, USN.

Coye #2 - 139

title of it was "Sea Power and the National Interest." Of course, it required quite a bit of research. I submitted it to the Naval Institute for the annual prize essay, but they sent back word that they had had a number of papers on the same subject. Of course, that was our assigned subject. I think I wrote another paper on "Submarines as Radar Picket Vessels," because off Okinawa when the radar picket destroyers were being sunk, it looked like a submarine could do a better job. So I wrote an article on that at the War College.

Q: I expected you to write an article on submarines.

Admiral Coye: Yes.

Q: And your main contribution was your knowledge of submarines, I should suspect.

Admiral Coye: Yes.

Q: I've forgotten how many people attend the War College courses at one time.

Admiral Coye: There again, it was similar to the Staff College in that we had a large number of Army and Air Force people, plus State Department. I don't know whether we had CIA or not, but we had in the class maybe 100 or something like that.

Q: Oh, that many? Were they doing war games at that time?

Admiral Coye: No, they didn't have their war game set up then.

Q: But you did enjoy it?

Admiral Coye: Yes, I enjoyed mostly the lectures and the library the most.

Q: You don't fail or pass there, do you? You just attend and that's it?

Admiral Coye: You can.

Q: Could anyone ever fail it?

Admiral Coye: Well, they give you a fitness report that says how you've done, but I never heard of anybody really failing the course. They wouldn't give it to you again or something if you failed.

Q: The next two years you were in a very important and I'm sure it was a complicated staff relating to the Second Fleet and the Striking Force of the Atlantic and NATO exercises. I would be happy to have you describe everything you can about those things you accomplished within that two-year period of 1955 to 1957.

Admiral Coye: Well, I was pleased to get orders to the Second Fleet and Striking Fleet Atlantic. They are basically the same fleet, except one has a NATO hat and the other is a U.S. hat.

The Second Fleet, of course, comprises all the ships in the Atlantic Fleet. It has headquarters in Norfolk. My first job on there was operations officer, which meant really planning the operations of practically the whole Atlantic Fleet, because all the ships unless they were assigned in overhaul or assigned to their type commanders for some specific reason came under the jurisdiction of the Second Fleet. We were responsible for all their training and all their exercises.

As Striking Fleet Atlantic, we were responsible under our NATO hat for exercises which included the British fleets that were assigned to NATO, and any NATO ships in the Atlantic were assigned to us. For these exercises, the major one of which was Strike Back, the Strike Fleet Commander and the staff would go aboard a ship. We had several of these exercises. One year we went on the New Jersey, and on the others we went on the Northampton.

In preparation for Strike Back, the staff embarked in a ship and cruised to the Norwegian Sea. This was primarily to test the communications in the area. We tried to simulate the conditions we would have when we had the entire Striking Fleet with us. We made one cruise in the New Jersey which was a most comfortable ship in the heavy seas that could be encountered in the northern waters. It was well equipped as a flagship. I recall during a port visit in Oslo, Norway, we gave a formal dinner for the Prince of Norway in the flag cabin. The New Jersey, of course, had beautiful silver service and proper dinner service. On another cruise, and during the actual Strike Back exercise, the staff embarked in Northampton. The Northampton (not the original Northampton which was sunk in World War II) was designed as a amphibious command ship---so it was fitted with lots of communication facilities, a large CIC, and two flag quarters (one for the admiral and one for a general). Thus, as a flagship, it was superior to New Jersey but, of course, New Jersey offered other advantages such as superior seakeeping, an almost infinite range, heavy firepower, better damage control, and the ability to refuel the escorts.

Most of the exercises were conducted up in the Norwegian Sea, because our job was to keep the Russian submarines from attacking our fleets. It was a real challenging assignment. A lot was involved in the planning of these exercises. We would have to make trips to coordinate with the NATO commanders in Europe. So we made several trips, I remember, to Paris headquarters to the supreme high commander. It involved trips up to Norway, to CinCNorth, who was a NATO commander, and of course to England to coordinate with the British. So the planning of these exercises really took more time than the actual exercises themselves.

After a short while, in addition to being operations officer, I was promoted up to being deputy chief of staff for plans, operations, and readiness. This was really a large staff. You had to have a large staff for all the various functions that we performed. My first commander was Admiral Wellborn.* He is one of the most able commanders I've ever seen or known. A very smart man. He was natural leader and the whole staff idolized him. He grasped the big picture, yet paid attention to details. Many times I would take orders to him for his signature and they would come back with paper clips on various pages that needed corrections or could be improved. Both he and his charming wife had a hobby of sports cars, and he had one of the early Porsches. He kept himself in top physical condition and could beat most anybody on the staff at handball. He would have made an ideal CNO.

Then in the latter part of the tour we had Admiral Pirie as the commander.** Admiral Pirie was a most capable leader. He was an aviator, whereas Admiral Wellborn had been a surface ship sailor. I think that the powers that be felt for the actual conduct of Strike Back that an aviator should be at the helm since so many carriers and aircraft were involved. Admiral Pirie was a more dashing type and left more of the details to the staff. In any event, with the planning of Admiral Wellborn, and the brilliant execution by Admiral Pirie, exercise Strike Back was a success.

---

*Vice Admiral Charles Wellborn, Jr., USN.
**Vice Admiral Robert B. Pirie, USN.

Coye #2 - 144

This was a large-scale exercise, and lots of ships and hundreds of airplanes were involved in this.

Q: Any amphibious?

Admiral Coye: No, I don't recall the amphibious part.

Q: Ships, airplanes, and submarines?

Admiral Coye: Yes.

Q: How long did it take? You said the planning took longer than the exercise.

Admiral Coye: The exercise would last usually about three weeks, as I remember it, three or four weeks, I think. It took time to get up north and get up the Norwegian Sea, to run the exercise and get back. I'd say about three weeks or so for the exercises themselves.

Q: How many ships were involved? Do you recall?

Admiral Coye: Oh, probably between 100 and 200 ships. They were the largest scale exercises.

Q: Were they all NATO? Various nationalities?

Admiral Coye: All assigned to NATO for that period, yes.

Q: They were various nationalities?

Admiral Coye: Various nationalities, yes.

Q: Where were you?

Admiral Coye: I was in the flagship, the <u>Northampton</u>.

Q: Oh, you mentioned that, yes. Did the Russians give you any trouble?

Admiral Coye: No, they didn't, strange to say. This was, of course, quite a while ago and as I understand now, the Russian planes come out when we conduct similar exercises and enter into the exercises. But we didn't have any problems with the Russians.

Q: But I would imagine you felt that was really a rewarding assignment.

Admiral Coye: Yes, operationally I think I learned a lot about how to operate ships from that job.

Q: There probably would never be a large one unless there was an actual breaking of peace, which I hope doesn't ever happen. But I can't imagine a larger operation in peacetime.

Admiral Coye: No, there wouldn't be.

Q: Do they have these regularly now?

Admiral Coye: I know the English don't have as many ships as they used to. Our carriers are more deployed to the Indian Ocean and whatnot, so we can't afford to send as many carriers up on this type of thing. I don't think the operations are actually as large right now when they have them. I think they only have them, but I'm not positive, about every other year now.

Q: But there's no effort to send troops up there? You said no amphibious.

Admiral Coye: I don't remember any amphibious.

Q: Your planning related to the airplanes and the ships and submarines.

Admiral Coye: Right.

Q: How large would your plans be?

Coye #2 - 147

Admiral Coye: Oh, I'd say an op order with its annexes is probably six or eight inches thick.

Q: You had to make copies for hundreds of ships?

Admiral Coye: Yes, it was a big operation.

Q: How many people would you have helping you prepare those op orders and the annexes?

Admiral Coye: Oh, I probably had about 30 or 35, somewhere around there.

Q: And there was always the time pressure to get them out on time and get them to the people so that everybody got the word.

Admiral Coye: Yes.

Q: Now, did you know what particular significance "Strike Back" had? Did it have a particular significance other than just the name itself?

Admiral Coye: No. In one of our early conferences, we were trying to decide what to name this exercise and as I recall, I was the one that suggested "Strike Back," because it had a good connotation. We figured it might scare the Russians a little bit to know that we were ready to strike back if we had to.

Q: And of course they were aware? You could not help having been aware that this operation was being planned and conducted?

Admiral Coye: Oh yes. They knew that.

Q: Do you think it accomplished anything?

Admiral Coye: Oh yes, I'm sure it did. It had a lot of training in those waters. It's not the best weather in the world up there, though there are some nice days. But it's rough up there. It accomplished quite a bit.

Q: You were in the Norwegian Sea?

Admiral Coye: Yes.

Q: I don't want to leave out anything that's an important segment of your career. I don't want us to leave out anything that should be included.

Admiral Coye: No, I think that covers it pretty well.

Q: You then went back to a different climate entirely in January of

Coye #2 - 149

1958, if I'm correct. You went back to the Pacific?

Admiral Coye: Right. My tour was about up in Second Fleet, and BuPers offered me command of a cruiser, the Rochester. I said I'd be glad to take the Rochester. It was one of the newer cruisers, actually, CA-124. It was a single-stack heavy cruiser, one of the prettiest cruisers that was ever designed. It was a flagship for Commander Seventh Fleet. At the time, it was deployed out to WestPac, so I went out there and took command of it.

Commander Seventh Fleet at the time was Admiral Beakley, a very distinguished aviator.* It was, of course, the biggest ship I had ever had command of. I found that it handled about like the other ships; you put right full rudder on and it goes right and left rudder goes left.

Q: That was convenient.

Admiral Coye: I had a good crew on there, too. Admiral Beakley was a very fine man to work for. His staff, of course, was on board, and we got along fine. If he wanted to be at a certain place at a certain time, as long as you were there at that time, then everything was fine. And we never were late, so we had a good relationship.

Also, my experience on Strike Fleet staff was helpful as I knew

---

*Vice Admiral Wallace M. Beakley, USN.

what an admiral expected of his flag captain. Admiral Beakley never interfered with the way I maneuvered the ship. Our cabins were adjacent with a door in between. This was mostly open and in the evenings we often got together to swap sea stories. The only time that I remember he spoke a cross word to me was after a general quarters drill when the water got shut off from his shower while he was showering. Needless to say, after this I assigned one of the ensigns to make certain that the valve to the admiral's shower was left open during general quarters.

Admiral Beakley did much to promote goodwill in the Philippines and as I recall we had the Philippine President on board for one of the exercises.

Q: Where was it actually in the Western Pacific?

Admiral Coye: Let's see. Japan and the Philippines. I don't remember all the ports. I joined it in Yokosuka and we went to Sasebo and Nagoya and down to Manila.

They conducted an amphibious exercise down in the Philippines. Then, after we came back from WestPac, the ship went to navy yard overhaul in San Francisco.

Q: Before you come back, had Vietnam had any effect by this time?

Admiral Coye: No. At that time there were three cruisers that

Coye #2 - 151

deployed as Seventh Fleet flagship, and they took turns relieving each other. So there was always one out in the Western Pacific. When we left, another cruiser---I think it was the Los Angeles---relieved us and we transferred the Seventh Fleet staff to that. Then we headed back for San Francisco.

Q: Do we want to add anything to that?

Admiral Coye: No, I don't think so. We went through a usual navy yard overhaul. Then we came down to San Diego and conducted refresher training, which you always do after a navy yard overhaul. You get a lot of gun shooting and exercises. It was very impressive to fire the guns, because of course it had those nine 8-inch guns and a whole slew of 5-inch guns and a lot of 40s and 20s. It was fun, really, shooting at targets with them.

Q: How far offshore would you be to do this?

Admiral Coye: We did it off San Clemente Island.

Q: I hope you were shooting in the opposite direction.

Admiral Coye: Yes. We did well in the refresher training, and then we went up to Long Beach and that was, of course, our home port. We operated some out of there. Command of a ship is in my opinion the

Coye #2 - 152

best and most rewarding job in the Navy. Personally I would rather have a ship command than be CNO. The Rochester was a fine ship and we had an excellent crew. It was, of course, much more maneuverable than the Fulton and we had more time cruising at sea. Of course it couldn't dive like a submarine but I encouraged several of the smart young ensigns to apply for submarine school. They did well in submarines and later had their own commands. About that time, my year had expired. It went by all too quickly. You don't get to keep cruiser commands very long.

Q: There are not enough of them to go around.

Admiral Coye: That's true.

Q: Who relieved you?

Admiral Coye: A submarine officer, Bob Ward, R.E.M. Ward, class of '35.[*] He's since died. He was a very capable officer, though. He later got promoted to flag rank.

Q: When did your flag rank come?

Admiral Coye: Not until 1961.

---

[*]Captain Robert E.M. Ward, USN.

Coye #2 - 153

Q: Because I can see all of these jobs leading up to that.

Admiral Coye: Yes.

Q: You've had a wonderful variety of experiences.

Admiral Coye: Yes. I hadn't had any jobs in Washington, so BuPers said, "You've got to go to Washington." I didn't particularly object to going to Washington, but it so happened I never had any job there, so then I got ordered back to OpNav.

Q: I have DCNO Fleet Operations and Readiness; is that right?

Admiral Coye: Right.

Q: And that would have been in January of 1959, just after the end of your year tour on the Rochester.

Admiral Coye: Yes.

Q: And what was your job there?

Admiral Coye: Oh, I started out in OP-341. That was a section of a division back there. That was sort of a catch-all job, it seemed to me. Anything they didn't know what to do, they gave it to them. But anyway, that was in OP-34, basically, and that was called Strike Warfare Division. It used to be the Readiness Division, and they reorganized and called it Strike Warfare. Then in the same division I had the Air Defense because as you know, there's a lot of politicking going on back in Washington. The ASW people were getting more money than the Air Defense people were, so we changed the name from Air Defense to Anti-Air Warfare and that's what it is today. It was sort of a catch-all division. That included Air Defense, and we represented the amphibious people, the surface people, and everybody except the aviators. They had their own DCNO.

Q: And when you say you represented them, what do you mean by that?

Admiral Coye: I mean that when they had problems in the fleet that they wanted handled back in Washington, they'd send them back to OpNav, and then OpNav would funnel them out to whoever could answer that letter. We got the ones related to surface ships, amphibious ships, and antiair warfare.

Q: Mostly administration again?

Admiral Coye: Mostly administration, but you were also fighting the battle of the budget, you know. Every year you'd have your five-year plans to make and have to tell Congress how much money you needed to buy what ships and what equipment. It was an interesting job. We used to say we worked half-days back there, 7:00 to 7:00.

Q: I've heard that those jobs are long and demanding.

Admiral Coye: They are demanding. It's not really too satisfying, really. You're mainly pushing papers around. I'd rather push ships around than push papers around, but it was a very enlightening experience. I enjoyed it, but I'd rather have been out at sea, actually.

Q: I think you had to have that in your career to get selected for admiral.

Admiral Coye: Yes, I think you're probably right, because I can't think of anybody offhand. There's probably been some who've been selected who didn't have a tour in Washington.

Q: But it seems to me that your personality is such that you've never had any problems with anyone. Is that correct?

Admiral Coye: No, I can't think of any real serious problems with anybody, no.

Q: Nobody got mad at you?

Admiral Coye: No.

Q: At least not the right people---or the wrong people, depending on how you look at that.

Admiral Coye: No.

Q: But that was a two-year period.

Admiral Coye: Yes.

Q: Exhausting and demanding?

Admiral Coye: Yes. Well, the best part of it was the Pentagon Athletic Club. I used to go every lunch hour and catch a swim in their pool. That was a big event of the day. But I made a lot of friends in the Pentagon and, as I say, I'm sure that other people got to know me from being back there at the Pentagon, and it was a good experience.

Q: Well, let's see now. I don't want to leave anything out in the DCNO.

Admiral Coye: In the same division there, from being Anti-Air Warfare, I was promoted to what they call 34B. That's really the assistant division chief of the Strike Warfare. I had that job for about the last year I was there. They had OP-34, and then I was OP-34B. That's theoretically a promotion.

Q: That was one of the top jobs, right?

Admiral Coye: Right. The Deputy CNO was Admiral Beakley again, who had had the Seventh Fleet, so he and I were good friends, and I could feel free to go in and discuss problems with him.

Q: That seems to me very important.

Admiral Coye: Yes.

Q: Well, your goal is accomplished, because about the time you were detached as you became rear admiral or you became rear admiral and detached or ...

Admiral Coye: No, I was selected and then detached.

Q: In September of 1961?

Admiral Coye: Right.

Q: And then tell me where you were.

Coye #2 - 158

Admiral Coye: Then I went to Guam as Commander Naval Forces Marianas. I relieved a classmate, Wally Wendt.* That was a most interesting tour. I don't know how familiar you are with Guam. I had an area the size of the United States, but the land in it was about the size of Rhode Island. On Guam we had at least a dozen commands: the air station, the naval base, the ship repair facility, the naval ordnance facility, the hospital, the dental. I had about a dozen commands that came under me there to coordinate. Then I had the responsibility for more or less the protection of the trust territory. The trust territory was under the United Nations, but that involved all the islands from Truk, the Carolines, Palau, Saipan, all those. I had several ships that would go around and administer to the natives, giving them medical treatment and things like that.

Q: Was Eniwetok included in that?

Admiral Coye: No, Eniwetok wasn't in that area.

Q: Because the job was Commander Naval Forces Marianas, wasn't it?

Admiral Coye: Right.

Q: With additional duty as Commander in Chief of the Pacific

---

*Rear Admiral Waldemar F.A. Wendt, USN.

Coye #2 - 159

Representing Marianas and Bonins.

Admiral Coye: While up near the Bonins I had an interesting little island called Chi Chi Jima. Chi Chi Jima had been originally manned by survivors of whaling ships, Americans. These survivors had been there and they had established this little town there called Yankee Town. Then when the Japanese came along, why, they took them all back to Japan during the war and manned the islands themselves and heavily fortified it. But after the war, we brought these people back to Chi Chi Jima, and we kept a detachment up there of a lieutenant commander and a lieutenant and a doctor, I think, and about a dozen Marines, because we kept nuclear guided missile reloads for one of our first guided missile submarines up there. So this was up near the Bonins, and one of the most interesting places there. The natives, as I say, were like New Englanders, because they were all descendents of these whaling people.

Q: How many would be there?

Admiral Coye: Oh, maybe 20 or more.

Q: Oh, just a few.

Admiral Coye: Just a few, yes. They had intermarried, sort of. They had married some Japanese. There was quite a mixture. One of these

Coye #2 - 160

whalers had apparently been a Negro, so some of them were sort of a darkish tinge. But they had American names. Washington was one I remember. Anyway, it was an interesting place and that was part of my command and I used to get up there and inspect. The only way you could get up there quickly was to take an amphibious plane and land in the harbor. To give them something to do, we had them fish, and once a month we'd send a little ship up there to take their fish and bring it back to Guam and feed that fish to the Philippine laborers that we had there in Guam. So it was quite a cycle.

Q: I know it's an enormous area. You said it's the size of the United States and very little land. But how many places would your ships actually have to call on?

Admiral Coye: Oh, in the islands there? Probably 25 or 30 or so little islands and atolls.

Q: Were there people on all of these islands?

Admiral Coye: Yes, on all the ones they stopped at.

Q: Did you go?

Admiral Coye: I went over to Truk, because I wanted to see Truk, having been off Truk during the war. I wanted to see that. That used to be a Japanese main base. I wanted to see what that looked like.

Q: From the land side.

Admiral Coye: Yes, from the land side. I went to a couple of the other islands, too, but mainly I couldn't really afford to get away from my headquarters too much. We had to worry about typhoons, because typhoons can come through there 12 months of the year.

The year I was there, we tracked 25 different typhoons. One of them, Typhoon Karen, went directly over the island and did an awful lot of damage. We had steady winds of 165 knots with gusts of 185.

Q: Oh, my.

Admiral Coye: That almost wiped us out. Another thing I was responsible for there was all the public works on the islands, all the roads and telephones and light and power. That all came under Commander Naval Forces Marianas.

Q: You had a whole city you were responsible for.

Admiral Coye: Yes. Then the Air Force had a command up in the northern part of the island, a SAC base. They kept a SAC division up there. At that time they were B-47s, and the SAC division commander was a general, General Kingsbury.* We became very close friends, because we were the only two flag officers within 1,000 miles or so. The closest neighbors we had were in the Philippines or back in Pearl Harbor. So we became very close friends. He'd take me up in his plane occasionally. He had his own personal B-47. If we had a submarine in (submarines stopped by there occasionally), I'd take him out for a ride in a submarine, things like that.

Q: How far away was he? You say he was on the other side.

Admiral Coye: He was up about 20 miles away. It's not a very big island.

Q: I think I cut you off when you were talking about the typhoon that almost wiped you out. Did you want to describe more of that?

Admiral Coye: Well, I had already had my relief ordered and was due to leave when this typhoon came through on November 11th and 12th of 1962.** As I say, it did an extreme amount of damage to the island, but we had warning of this, so we were able to warn everybody. So the loss of life was only about eight natives who refused to take shelter. None of the armed forces were injured.

---

*Brigadier General William C. Kingsbury, USAF.
**Typhoon Karen.

Q: What about the buildings?

Admiral Coye: Oh, the buildings were pretty much damaged. We had a lot of Quonset huts there left over from World War II. A good many of them were blown away. My headquarters had been built typhoon-proof, so that was all right. My quarters were badly damaged. The naval hospital was badly damaged. Oh, there was a lot of damage. I have a lot of pictures if sometime you want to take a look at them.

Q: Was your family with you?

Admiral Coye: Yes, Betty was with me and Sally. They took shelter in the naval hospital. I, of course, had to stay at the headquarters. It was quite an experience.

Q: Must have been. Speaking of typhoons, tell me about the weather in Guam. How would you describe it? What were the seasons?

Admiral Coye: Oh, Guam had four seasons. They had the dry part of the dry season, the wet part of the dry season, the dry part of the wet season and the wet part of the wet season.

Q: A lot of wet seasons.

Admiral Coye: A lot of wet seasons, yes.

Q: Did it pour torrentially part of every day?

Admiral Coye: No, there would be some days when it was dry, but there would be other days when it'd be raining all day, yes. It wasn't too bad. I personally don't mind the tropics; I like the warm weather. The rain is warm there, so it doesn't bother you.

Q: You dry off in a hurry?

Admiral Coye: Yes. I always used to say, "I don't mind being cold and I don't mind being wet, but I don't like to be cold and wet."

Q: Did you have any problems there in your various commands?

Admiral Coye: No, they were all very cooperative. I really didn't have any problems.

Q: I suspect that was because of the character and personality of the command.

Admiral Coye: I don't know. One interesting thing did happen there. The Japanese, as you know, treated the Guamanians pretty rough during World War II and murdered a lot of their people. Practically every family had had at least one member killed by the Japanese.

Coye #2 - 165

Q: When they came ashore there?

Admiral Coye: Yes. So while I was there, the Japanese got permission from the State Department to send a team down to write the history of the war from the Japanese viewpoint on Guam. This plane arrived with big meatballs on it and whatnot. It was the first Japanese plane that had ever come into Guam since World War II, and they had a general and a couple of colonels. We showed them all around the islands. They were making notes, you know, doing an oral history of World War II. I was a little concerned that maybe the natives might do something to these Japs, but they didn't. My chief steward, who was a Guamanian, assured me before they came that the Guamanians were a very forgiving people and there would be no episodes, and there weren't.

Q: I was expecting you to say that there was trouble.

Admiral Coye: No, no trouble.

Q: They'd have to be very forgiving, I would think.

Admiral Coye: Yes.

Q: Well, that was interesting--oral history from the Japanese viewpoint. That's really something. But Vietnam, I know, was happening.

Coye #2 - 166

Admiral Coye: It was just starting, yes. We were just starting to get special troops coming through there, communication troops. I remember we had one plane that came in carrying a company who were going to operate. It was some sort of communication company. It came through Guam, and on the way from Guam to the Philippines it was lost. We conducted an extensive search for that plane. I forget how many thousands of man hours we had trying to find that plane. We never did find it, but coincidentally, the plane that was carrying their equipment was coming through, and it came through by way of Alaska, and it also crashed. So we suspected that there was sabotage on that plane.

Q: On both of them?

Admiral Coye: On both of them, yes, because this was a highly trained company of communication experts and their equipment on their way out to Vietnam.

Q: It's a dumb question, but who would have sabotaged it?

Admiral Coye: Oh, the North Vietnamese, I guess.

Q: I wonder how they would get to it?

Admiral Coye: I don't know. But they investigated it. This was a

Coye #2 - 167

Flying Tiger plane with 104 people aboard.

Q: That's the first plane? And the second one crashed as well?

Admiral Coye: The second one crashed as well.

Q: From Guam to Vietnam, there were many, many planes going and coming. That was their base. But was that after you were there?

Admiral Coye: No, it was just starting when I was there.

Q: You said it was just starting. You spoke of these two planes. But I remember so many planes travelling so far with Guam as their headquarters and carrying big loads of bombs.

Admiral Coye: That's right. That was the B-52s. When I was there, we had B-47s there. But later on they had the B-52s, and they would start there. That was their base and they'd bomb from Guam.

Q: And that was after your tour had ended.

Admiral Coye: Yes.

Q: So many of your latter duties are such big tours that they have to get time for other people to have their duties, so they didn't last too long, I presume.

Admiral Coye: Yes.

Q: But you did enjoy that?

Admiral Coye: I did enjoy that.

Q: I'm sure you did a very good job for your country at that point. I know that the command you had was so large in the Marianas. So you want to pursue anything further about the trust territories or incidents that happened there or any other items that might be pertinent?

Admiral Coye: No, it was a real interesting experience and, as I say, I thoroughly enjoyed it. I had nice quarters until they got blown away, but the quarters I lived in were built for Admiral Nimitz in World War II.* They overlooked the Pacific Ocean toward the Philippines, high up on a cliff. Admiral Nimitz was still interested in them. He used to write me hand-written letters wanting to know how things were going and how the various flowers were and how the Guamanian people were. He thought a lot of the Guamanians. That part

---

*Fleet Admiral Chester W. Nimitz, USN, Commander in Chief Pacific Fleet and Pacific Ocean Areas had his headquarters in Pearl Harbor much of World War II. He moved to Guam in January 1945 in order to be nearer the combat areas.

of the duty was most interesting. I enjoyed Guam very much.

Q: I thought it was interesting that you told me when we weren't taping that even as late as this time there were people coming out trying to find Amelia Earhart.

Admiral Coye: Yes, of course it's always been a mystery as to what happened to Amelia. One of the theories was that the Japanese had rescued her and taken her to their headquarters on Saipan and that she was buried on Saipan. We had one newspaper reporter come out there, Fred Goerner, who wrote a book called The Search for Amelia Earhart in which he pursued this theory, and he did dig up some bones, but they were never conclusively proven to be those of Amelia Earhart or Fred Noonan.[*]

Saipan had had an interesting history. Originally, a long time ago, before World War II, it had been German territory and then Japanese, and now it was a trust territory more or less administered by the Americans. So the people on there really didn't know who to trust or who to talk to. You could find people on there who said that they remembered seeing an American woman at that time. But they might have said anything they thought you wanted them to say.

Q: Was the implication that the Japanese had killed her?

---

[*]Fred Goerner, The Search for Amelia Earhart (Garden City, New York: Doubleday & Co., Inc., 1966). Admiral Coye is mentioned a number of times in Goerner's book.

Admiral Coye: That she had either been killed or had died.

Q: Of wounds?

Admiral Coye: Some cause, possibly disease.

Q: I think that's interesting. Anything more about Saipan?

Admiral Coye: Of course, Saipan and Guam both now have become tourist centers, primarily for the Japanese. The Japanese have built hotels on Guam. When I was there, there weren't any hotels on Guam and there weren't any on Saipan. But now I understand there are fairly modern hotels. I've never been back there, but the Japanese run tours from Japan to Gaum, package tours, and honeymoon couples come down there.

Q: Well, they're still ours, though, aren't they?

Admiral Coye: Guam is still ours, but I'm not sure about the trust territory. I think it was up for a plebiscite. I don't believe that's really ours anymore.

Q: The trust territories were kind of a new concept. How long had they been trust territories before you arrived? Were you the first?

Admiral Coye: No, I wasn't the first. They had been since

World War II.

Q: So it was a matter of 20 years, probably. Not quite, but some time. Did you have any trouble with that aspect of Guam, the fact of being responsible for the trust territories?

Admiral Coye: No, the high commissioner of the trust territory was a man named Will Goding.* He was a very capable man, and he and I got along fine together with no problems.

Q: Was he on Guam?

Admiral Coye: He was on Guam at first, and then later while I was there they moved his headquarters to Saipan, because Guam is not a part of the trust territory. So they moved his headquarters to the trust territory.

Q: I find it interesting that you haven't been back. Because it was such an important part of your life, I would think you would really want to go take a look.

Admiral Coye: Well, it's a long ways.

Q: Yes, it is. So should we leave that part of your life and go on

---
*M. Wilfred Goding.

to your next duty?

Admiral Coye: Yes, I think we can.

Q: Which, according to my notes, is Commander of Amphibious Group Three.

Admiral Coye: Right.

Q: Where was that?

Admiral Coye: Amphibious Group Three was based in San Diego. Actually the amphibious force in the Pacific was split into two amphibious groups, Amphibious Group One and Amphibious Group Three. Amphibious Group One was normally out in the Western Pacific, and Amphibious Group Three was in the Eastern Pacific. The ships would go back and forth. The ones from Amphibious Group Three would deploy and then they'd become ships in Amphibious Group One and vice versa. So basically, Amphibious Group Three was a training area for the amphibious forces, and we had all types of amphibious ships in there. They were divided up, of course, into squadrons. As I recall, we had three amphibious squadrons, and these included AKs and LSDs, LSTs, and they had the usual beach jumpers and the UDT types, SEAL teams. Of course, the amphibious base was here in Coronado. My headquarters were on one of the amphibious ships. Mostly it was on the El Dorado, but on occasion I'd go to an LPH, one of the helicopter carriers. But I was more or less always on a ship with my staff. I had a fairly large staff, because amphibious operations involved a lot of details and we worked very closely with the Marines. The Marines kept a Marine expeditionary force at Camp Pendleton. Periodically, we would run exercises with the Marines; we'd embark them on our ships and then go up to the beach off of Camp Pendleton and land them there and have exercises.

I remember we did one called Steel Gate, in which we made the landing at nighttime without any communications. That was an experiment, but it turned out very well and there were no casualties. We landed several thousand troops, all quietly. That was the main accomplishment of that year, as I recall.

Q: What do you mean without communications? Between the ships, between the shore and ships?

Admiral Coye: Between the shore and ships and between the boats going ashore; they couldn't use their radios. Radio silence was in order.

Q: I hope Camp Pendleton knew you were coming.

Admiral Coye: Yes.

Q: How large an exercise? When you say this amphibious task force and amphibious exercise, how many people are we talking about?

Admiral Coye: Oh, we're talking about several thousand people.

Q: And how many ships? Hundreds?

Admiral Coye: No, probably maybe ten ships or something like that. I don't remember exactly, but on that order.

Q: But anyway, it was a big affair, I think.

Admiral Coye: Yes.

Q: So you had that job, again, just a bit over a year, right?

Admiral Coye: Right.

Q: Have we covered that, do you think?

Admiral Coye: Yes, I think so.

Q: It sounds like such a big job.

Admiral Coye: Of course, aside from running exercises, why, I inspected ships under my command and gave them personnel inspections,

Coye #2 - 175

surprise inspections and things like that—a lot of administrative duties involved. That was the main thing.

Q: Did we mention that you went out to the Marianas as rear admiral?

Admiral Coye: Yes, I think we did.

Q: I hope so.

Admiral Coye: After I was selected, I went out as rear admiral. I didn't get paid as a rear admiral for quite a while.

Q: Yes, you said you were selected and promoted all around the period of late 1961.

Admiral Coye: Yes.

Q: Did you go out as rear admiral?

Admiral Coye: Yes.

Q: You didn't get paid that?

Admiral Coye: No, because I didn't make my number until later.

Coye #2 - 176

Q: Oh, I see. Well, at least you had the comfort of knowing that you were a rear admiral. And you were a year then at the amphibious command.

Admiral Coye: Right.

Q: And then you went for an actual tour of two years as deputy chief of staff to the Commander in Chief Allied Forces Southern Europe. I'm sure that was an interesting two years.

Admiral Coye: Yes, this was a NATO command based in Naples which combined the NATO commitments of Italy, Greece, and Turkey. My job there was deputy chief of staff for logistics and administration. The commander, CinCSouth, was four-star Admiral James Russell, Jim Russell, who was one of the outstanding officers that I've ever met or had occasion to work for. His nickname was "Gentleman Jim," and that was very apt, because he was in essence a real gentleman and a very smart gentleman. It took somebody with his ability to coordinate the Italians and the Greeks and the Turks.

Q: I can imagine. Especially the Greeks and the Turks.

Admiral Coye: Yes. When he retired he should have gone to be either ambassador to Greece or Turkey, because both sides loved him.

Coye #2 - 177

Q: That would be a neat accomplishment. You were in Naples?

Admiral Coye: Based in Naples. Our headquarters were out at a place called Bagnoli. We had a large staff, and the staff was comprised of Americans, Italians, Greek, and Turkish officers of all three services--the Army, Navy, and Air Force. We also had some English and French officers. This is the southern sector of NATO that we were responsible for. We had to coordinate many things. We had large-scale exercises which would be held maybe in Turkey. We'd go over and run those. Some exercises were in Greece. It was really quite an event over there.

Q: Can you describe some of the exercises, some of the events? What was the purpose and what did you accomplish?

Admiral Coye: The exercises are really hard to describe. Their basic purpose is to keep the Russians from coming into either Greece or Turkey or Italy. Some of them were landing force exercises, some of them were at-sea exercises.

Q: Were the aircraft under you? Were the aircraft carriers under you?

Admiral Coye: Yes, for the purposes of these exercises, the Sixth

Fleet would be operating under AFSouth.* As usual, there were many conferences. We had to go up to Paris to consult with the supreme commander up there. Then, of course, it involved conferences with the Turkish and the Greek people, too, so I did a lot of traveling in that job.

Q: Did you ever get into the Black Sea? Any of your exercises go there?

Admiral Coye: We didn't actually go in the Black Sea. I've been up through the Bosporus, though.

Q: At the Black Sea, of course, you would be in Russian territory.

Admiral Coye: Yes. Some of our exercises were conducted from a mountain there full of tunnels which were supposed to be nuclear bomb-proof. For some of our nuclear exercises, we'd go up and sit in that mountain for a while.

Q: When you say nuclear exercises ...

Admiral Coye: Well, when we were planning nuclear attacks and anticipating retaliatory attacks, we'd go up in these bomb-proof headquarters.

---
*AFSouth—Allied Forces Southern Europe.

Q: That was a war game of sorts?

Admiral Coye: A war game, yes.

Q: I hope it never happens.

Admiral Coye: Yes. The official language for the headquarters was English, which was fortunate. I studied some Italian, but I never became really proficient in it and even less proficient in Greek or Turkish. However, Betty became fairly fluent in Italian, and this was a big help in entertaining.

Q: Did they understand? Did they speak English?

Admiral Coye: Most of them spoke fair English. They didn't always understand, but they'd nod like they did.

Q: And that confuses you twice as much.

Admiral Coye: That general was recently captured—Dozier.[*] His counterpart was there. That was part of our area up in Northern Italy. That came under us, too. So I had been up there and knew all about where he was in that area.

---

[*] Brigadier General James L. Dozier, USA, was abducted by the Red Brigades guerrilla group at Verona, Italy 17 December 1981. He was rescued on 28 January 1982 by Italian police.

Coye #2 - 180

After Admiral Russell left, we had Admiral Griffin relieve him.[*]
He was also a very smart officer.

Q: They probably send their best over there for those NATO commands.

Admiral Coye: He had me do a job on reorganizing the staff. I conducted a survey and decided we had really too many people on the staff. So I eliminated a lot of jobs, including my own.

Q: That's one way to get detached.

Admiral Coye: Yes, that's one way to get detached.

Q: Why did you do that?

Admiral Coye: Well, it was overstaffed. We had all these Greeks and Turks and Italians and they really couldn't do the paper work that was involved, so we had a lot of Americans that really were doing the work on the staff.

Q: In other words, it was duplicated because they didn't understand the language, I presume.

Admiral Coye: So I thought, "Well, let's really make this a joint

---

[*]Admiral Charles Donald Griffin, USN.

staff and make people work." So I eliminated quite a few of the jobs.

Q: Americans, mostly?

Admiral Coye: Yes, mainly Americans.

Q: Did that make you popular?

Admiral Coye: Oh, I don't know how popular it made me.

Q: Well, I would imagine it would be very nice duty to be down in that part of the world for a year or so.

Admiral Coye: Yes, it's pleasant down there.

Q: Did they adopt your reorganization?

Admiral Coye: Pretty much, yes.

Q: Were there any problems relating to the Egyptians and the Israelis and the Middle East? Any problems when you were there?

Admiral Coye: No. I did take a leave and took a tour of the Middle East, but it wasn't in any official capacity. There weren't any problems.

Q: Did they come within your area?

Admiral Coye: No.

Q: The reason I was interested is that I can't remember when it happened (foolish, I guess), but at one time the Israelis shot a ship?

Admiral Coye: The *Liberty*, yes. That was after I was there.

Q: That was after your time. Because that's always been a difficult thing to get anyone to talk about.

Admiral Coye: Right.

Q: But that was after you were detached.

Admiral Coye: Yes.

Q: Do we have everything now?

Admiral Coye: I think so, yes. That was another interesting tour that I was very fortunate in.

Q: I think what you do is make them sound so easy. You make each job sound like it was easy.

Coye #2 - 183

Admiral Coye: Well, I don't know. They were interesting.

Q: I'm sure they were interesting. Well, sometimes I look at this, like the Marianas and you say it as though just anyone can do it, and I'm sure it took a particular skill and expertise which you have.

Admiral Coye: Well, I don't know.

Q: You wouldn't say that.

Admiral Coye: No.

Q: Well, that's all we can do.

Admiral Coye: That about covers it, I think.

Q: Now then, it says in February of 1966 you were ordered detached for duty as Commander Training Command Atlantic Fleet.

Admiral Coye: Right.

Q: Tell me about that.

Admiral Coye: Well, we left Naples. Actually, I had a little leave so Betty and Sally and I took a tour through Europe and rode back to the United States on the <u>United States</u>. That was a very interesting trip. Then I went to Norfolk where the headquarters for the training command is. That job was a challenging job.

The training command is responsible, of course, for all the training of the Atlantic Fleet. Our main jobs were the ships that came out of overhaul or the new ships. For that, we had Guantanamo where we would send the ships down for their intensive gunnery training and damage control and all sorts of exercises. In addition to that, I had training groups in Newport and Norfolk and Charlestown and Key West and Mayport. They did individual training with ships based in that area. Also, some of the schools came under my command.

At Dam Neck, where we did the antiair warfare training, that was under my command. In Key West we had the fleet sonar school. So it was a big command, but it was sort of spread around quite a bit. I had a fairly large staff, and we had to make a lot of trips to these various schools and go down to Guantanamo. I personally tried to go down to Guantanamo every time a large ship was going through its training phase. For a carrier or cruiser, I'd go down for their final battle problem.

Q: Were you the person who decided whether their training was up to the level that it should be?

Admiral Coye: Right.

Coye #2 - 185

Q: That was your responsibility?

Admiral Coye: Yes. I gave them their final mark of excellent or outstanding or failed or whatever. Then another thing that occurred while I was there was we started getting these bad carrier fires.*
Remember the Forrestal fire? So we did a lot of work on how to combat these fires, how to prevent them and then if they did get one, how to put them out. That was another thing that came under our command, all the fire fighting schools that they had. Those are quite exciting, those fire fighting schools. They put you in a compartment that's been set ablaze and give you a little, small hose with a nozzle and spray on it and tell you to put it out. It's a real thrill for the people doing it.

Q: Is that enlisted, officers, or both?

Admiral Coye: Both. Enlisted and officers.

Q: You'd be in there by yourself?

Admiral Coye: Yes. They'd have an instructor standing by in case something went wrong.

---

*The USS Oriskany suffered a fire during Vietnam War flight operations in 1966 and the USS Forrestal off Vietnam in 1967. The USS Enterprise had a flight deck fire and explosions near Hawaii in 1969.

Q: What did you ever conclude from these fires, the big fires on the carriers?

Admiral Coye: We developed some new fire fighting agents that were more effective, and since that time I don't believe they've had any real serious fires. Maybe one, but I don't think they have. At that time they recalled Admiral Russell, who had since retired--the one who had been in Naples. He was a famous aviator, and they recalled him back to duty to conduct a special panel on how to fight these fires. He came there in Norfolk with us and conferred with us.

Q: And your conclusion was that they needed better fire fighting materials, equipment, and chemicals?

Admiral Coye: Yes, and big ships now have them.

Q: That seems to have solved the problem, we hope.

Admiral Coye: Yes. These carriers are not only full of ammunition but they're full of jet fuel and whatnot. You just throw a match and you've got a big conflagration. So that was a real challenging job, that training command.

Q: When you had some of the large ships down at Guantanamo, did you ever find any of them unsatisfactory?

Coye #2 - 187

Admiral Coye: No, we had a good team down there in Guantanamo. They gave them two inspections—one when they first arrived and one when they were due to leave. Sometimes they would find them unsatisfactory when they came, but by the training we had given them, they always did well.

Q: Well, they were under you. The training at Guantanamo was under you, also, but you came down for the second inspection.

Admiral Coye: Yes, the final inspection. I wasn't there usually for the first inspection.

Q: But you never found any that didn't pass?

Admiral Coye: They all passed.

Q: I imagine that was an interesting job. I think training is vital, of course. I don't want to cut you off now if there's more.

Admiral Coye: At Dam Neck at the Antiair Warfare Center we were developing the NTDS, navy tactical data system. This was a new thing going into ships that linked all the naval ships by computers and linked all their radars together. That was another thing that was real interesting to see develop.

Coye #2 - 188

Q: That was the first use of computers between ships?

Admiral Coye: Pretty much between ships, yes, it was.

Q: Because individual ships, of course, had the radar and sonar and that sort of equipment.

Admiral Coye: Right. Of course all these computers had to be programmed. At Dam Neck we prepared the programs for the ships. As I say, it's a real advance in naval warfare.

Q: Is that what they call the software?

Admiral Coye: Yes.

Q: And who did the actual equipment? Who manufactured it?

Admiral Coye: I don't remember the name of the company.

Q: That takes a very high skill. You must have had new people in the Navy for this. I mean, people who were newly qualified. They would have had to go out, I'm guessing, to the manufacturer and learn how to do it and then come back. Were they naval officers who did this?

Admiral Coye: Naval officers and some civilians. They had to have the experience to write in the programs of what you do when a plane is approaching so far away and heading toward you—whether you shoot it down or what. Things like that depend on the experienced people, and they wrote the programs there. They'd also write them out here in the Pacific Fleet. There's a place out here over at NEL where they write programs, too, for the NTDS.

Q: I cannot conceive of the multiplicity of programs they would have to write for every conceivable situation.

Admiral Coye: Well, that's it. They're very extensive.

Q: There must be thousands.

Admiral Coye: Yes.

Q: Am I correct in thinking that?

Admiral Coye: I know that each ship that had this had to have its own program in it. It had to be compatible with the other ships.

Q: I've seen a little bit about how it reacts to, say, using these computers as a teaching aid. You have to have the software in it; you have to have the program in it or it's no good. Am I correct in relating it to this type of thing?

Admiral Coye: Yes, it's similar.

Q: Oh, on a very low level because this is like your great big commercial airlines.

Admiral Coye: Yes.

Q: They have this sort of thing in them now, too. But you can't get out what isn't in it, so it ...

Admiral Coye: Right. Garbage in, garbage out.

Q: Either one or both. Well, that's interesting. I didn't know that that was part of our ships' systems now. That's remarkable. How many ships carry this? What level, I mean?

Admiral Coye: All the carriers, of course, and the cruisers and some of the DDGs. All the newer ships.

Q: It is under destroyer guided missile, DDGs?

Admiral Coye: Yes, all the modern ships do, I think, pretty much have NTDS now.

Q: That's remarkable and very interesting. I'm glad that you brought

Coye #2 - 191

that up. That was of course in your training command. Had it been started before you got there?

Admiral Coye: Yes, it had.

Q: So your duty down there went clear up and down the East Coast and down to Cuba, right?

Admiral Coye: Right.

Q: Were you ready to retire then?

Admiral Coye: No.

Q: That was your last assignment, wasn't it?

Admiral Coye: My last assignment, yes. Including my Naval Academy time, I've had 39 years in the Navy. I enjoyed them all.

Q: Well, you're still awfully young. You're awfully young appearing now and that was how many years ago?

Admiral Coye: Fourteen.

Q: What have you been doing since you retired?

Coye #2 - 192

Admiral Coye: Well, we moved ...

Q: Excuse me, was your retirement ceremony very sad?

Admiral Coye: Well, we had ...

Q: Very weepy?

Admiral Coye: We three of us retired at the same time---Admiral Buie and Admiral Christopher and myself.* We all retired the same date there in Norfolk. So they made quite a ceremony out of it and had a parade and fly-over and everything.

Q: Did submarines come up and salute?

Admiral Coye: No. So after I retired, we had looked back on all the places we had lived and we decided that Coronado was the place we wanted to settle, though there was a big temptation to settle on the East Coast, because I like to sail and I like the Chesapeake. We almost retired to Annapolis, but the winters there are kind of cold and the summers are not all that good, some of them. So we came out here. I've never regretted it. We bought this house and have spent a lot of time fixing up the house. I had a boat and still have a boat.

---

*Rear Admiral Paul D. Buie, USN, and Rear Admiral Thomas A. Christopher, USN, both Naval Academy classmates of Admiral Coye.

Coye #2 - 193

Q: What kind of a boat?

Admiral Coye: I have a CAL-25 sloop that's a 25-foot sailboat.

Q: Where do you keep it?

Admiral Coye: At the Coronado Yacht Club. I became active in the yacht club and took various jobs there, all non-paying, of course. Then I've worked up from rear commodore to vice commodore to commodore of the Yacht Club. Now I'm a staff commodore, but still take an active interest in the Yacht Club more or less as one of their senior advisors. I've been a little active in the Red Cross as a director of the Coronado Red Cross. I took an electronics course and built that television there.

Q: Did you?

Admiral Coye: Yes.

Q: You did?

Admiral Coye: Yes.

Q: Oh, my! You didn't build the whole thing.

Admiral Coye: Yes, I built the whole thing.

Q: I have to say that's a beautiful piece of equipment.

Admiral Coye: Yes.

Q: Did you do the case and everything?

Admiral Coye: I did the case too, yes. I built a hi-fi. So I've managed to keep busy.

Q: You've also maintained your interest in music.

Admiral Coye: I finally decided that I ought to take lessons, so I'm taking lessons now once a month on the organ.

Q: And you've also made other pieces of furniture.

Admiral Coye: Yes.

Q: This table on which we're working?

Admiral Coye: I didn't make this table, no.

Q: Not this table.

Admiral Coye: I made that bookcase over there. But now I've run out of pieces of furniture to make. And I work in the garden. Betty does most of the work, but I do the heavy trimming. And we take trips. It's been an interesting time.

Q: You speak of coming out here. I know you have family. Let's get Beth last because I want to talk about her a little bit.

Admiral Coye: My youngest child, daughter Sally, is a school teacher. Shortly after I retired she entered college. She went to Occidental College in the Los Angeles area. Then she's taught for a while at La Jolla Country Day School. She's taught over in Portugal for a year at a private American school. Now she's back in Coronado where she is with the Chapman College administering programs to sailors and officers from the amphibious base and North Island Air Station. She also teaches adult education at a local high school, French and English as a second language. She's a very busy and energetic young lady. She lives in an apartment here in Coronado.

My son, Johnny ...

Q: Is he number three?

Admiral Coye: He's number two; he's in the middle.

Q: No, no, but I mean you're a junior and he's ...

Admiral Coye: Yes, he's three. He went to the Naval Academy and he used to have to sound off as J.S. Coye, III (aye, aye, aye). He was at the Naval Academy for about two and a half years, and then he got out because he got a medical survey because he has asthma problems. So he went to the University of Arizona, graduated, and then went into various businesses basically as a salesman for construction products. He was with Owens Corning Fiberglas and Simons, which makes concrete forms for bridges and buildings and things. He did very well. As a matter of fact, in his last job with Simons, he was the West Coast manager and they wanted him to come back to their home office which I think is in Toledo or someplace like that. But he didn't want to go back to Toledo, so he said he was going into business for himself. So he bought and started a camera shop in a new market area, a new shopping center up near Tiburon in Marin County. Of course, Marin County is one of the wealthiest counties in the United States, and he's done very well. He's got the Leica dealership up there is is doing extremely well. He has three children, Christopher, Joshua, and a new baby daughter, Lindsey. We just took Christopher and Joshua on a trip to Hawaii last summer. They're doing well.

Q: Now come to your middle child and your older of two daughters whose name is ...

Admiral Coye: Beth is the oldest.

Q: Oh, I thought John was the oldest. Oh, Beth is the oldest.

Admiral Coye: Beth is the oldest. Beth, of course, went to Wellesley and graduated. Then the following year she went into the WAVES and had a very successful career in the WAVES. Part of the time she was in intelligence and she was in recruiting duty. Her last job out here was in personnel---PSA, they call it---Personnel and Support Activity.

Q: She was a commanding officer?

Admiral Coye: Yes. They are responsible for all the personnel records and the financial records of people that were attached in training center and some of the other areas, a naval base, I believe. She had about 200 people working for her.

Q: Where was her office?

Admiral Coye: It was over at NTC. Then she retired after 21 years. I think if she had stayed on she probably would have been selected for captain, but she retired before the board met.

Q: Why didn't she stay on?

Admiral Coye: I don't know if she was disappointed in the way that women were being treated. As you've read her articles in the Naval

Institute, she has always thought that the women should get a better deal in the Navy.*

Q: I was wondering if that's why she retired.

Admiral Coye: Yes.

Q: And in what respect did she think they should get a better deal?

Admiral Coye: Well, I think promotion-wise, she felt that they were technically line officers 1100, but they didn't have all the same opportunities that the other 1100 officers did.** Yet they were competing with them.

Q: On the selection board?

Admiral Coye: On the selection board.

Q: Which has made it impossible competition, in a way, if you're talking about sea duty.

Admiral Coye: Yes.

---

*Commander Beth F. Coye, USN, "We've Come a Long Way, But...", U.S. Naval Institute Proceedings, July 1979, pages 41-49.
**1100 is the designator for unrestricted line officers who do not have a specialized warfare qualification.

Coye #2 - 199

Q: So you think that's why she retired. Also, she had also wanted to have a business of her own, which she now has.

Admiral Coye: Yes, I think looking back on it she enjoyed her Navy career.

Q: I was interested in what your reaction is about women in the Navy. I gather I know the answer; however, you certainly grew up in an all-man Navy and you didn't serve with women until when?

Admiral Coye: Oh, in Naples we had WAVES. Sally Watlington was there.* Do you know Sally?

Q: No.

Admiral Coye: She was on the staff in AFSouth. She's the one I predict is going to be the next woman admiral. She just left a command here as a captain. She's still young yet, but she was early selected for captain. I think she'll be the next admiral.

Q: Well, I wish her well. What is your feeling about women in the Navy? What is your feeling about them being treated fairly?

Admiral Coye: Well, I'm not so sure that they should go to sea. I

---
*Ensign Sarah J. Watlington, USN.

personally, on a submarine I don't know whether I'd like to have women on board or not. I think there are lots of jobs in the Navy that women can do just as well as men. Like this little gal I met the other day who is a jet mechanic out here on North Island. She was proud of what she was doing and from what I gather, she's just as good a mechanic as the man next to her is. Jobs like that are fine. I think as far as being aviators, I think that's probably all right. I read recently where one of the recent Academy graduates who went into aviation was killed, but there again, to fly a plane and particularly a single place plane, there wouldn't be any conflict between a man and a woman.

Q: Well, in physical skill.

Admiral Coye: Physical skill, yes.

Q: Physical qualifications.

Admiral Coye: The average job on board---well, as far as the average job on board ship doesn't really involve a lot of physical effort anymore. I mean, it used to be that you had to shovel coal and load the 16-inch shells.

Q: And scrape off the barnacles.

Admiral Coye: Yes, things like that don't happen anymore. So I think the women could be just as well qualified.

Q: What do you think about women going to Annapolis and becoming officers?

Admiral Coye: Well, I really think that in talking with you, you said that the Navy spends a lot of money putting somebody through the Academy and they're going to be career naval officers. Maybe that money ought to be better spent on men. But I don't have any real ...

Q: Well, don't take my feeling on it. I'm just interested in yours.

Admiral Coye: No, I think it's probably all right, because there are a lot of jobs in the Navy that require Academy education that can be done by women, so why not send them?

Q: It is a fairer thing to say that if women are going to serve in an equal capacity then they should have the same training?

Admiral Coye: Yes.

Q: I suppose it comes to that.

Admiral Coye: Yes.

Q: Is that a fair statement?

Admiral Coye: Yes, that's a fair statement. Now you look at the recent selection boards and you'll find that the percentage of the officers from the Academy being selected isn't much greater and in some cases not as great as the ones who came from OCS, the AV Cads and things like that and ROTC. So the Academy isn't ...

Q: Isn't the only basis for training.

Admiral Coye: The only basis for training. I think in Beth's article she had a lot of good points and I agree, I'd say, with most of them.

Q: Well, I've appreciated your comments. Is there anything that you feel you want to add now? We are pretty much at the finish.

Admiral Coye: No, I'd just like to say that I enjoyed my 39 years in the Navy and if I had my life to live over, I'd do it again. I'd like to thank you for your excellent questioning and preparation for this interview. You've done a fine job, Etta Belle.

Q: Well, in return, I would say that I'm sure the Navy is very fortunate to have you, and I've enjoyed seeing you. I hope that my questions were helpful. That's what I'm for. At the end, I have mentioned it before, but just because sometimes at the windup people see it better, I want them to know that the patrol reports are declassified and they are available at the submarine museum at the submarine base at Groton, Connecticut. Also, the track charts are also available but we're not sure where. Is that right?

Admiral Coye: That's right.

Q: So I thank you very much for your graph on the map.* That is very helpful.

---

*The map showing the patrols of the USS <u>Silversides</u> while Admiral Coye was in command is maintained in his file in the oral history office of the Naval Institute.

Index

to

Biography

of

Rear Admiral John S. Coye, Jr.

U. S. Navy (Retired)

Amphibious Warfare
    Coye involved in exercises as amphibious group commander in mid-1960s, pp. 172-175.

Antisubmarine Warfare
    See: Operational Development Force

Armed Forces Staff College
    Coye attends shortly after unification of armed services in late 1940s, pp. 126-127.

Beakley, Wallace M., Vice Admiral, USN (USNA, 1924)
    Distinguished aviator who was fine person to work for as Commander Seventh Fleet in 1950s, pp. 149-150; as Deputy CNO, p. 157.

Cater, Charles J., Lieutenant Commander, USN (USNA, 1922)
    Very capable commanding officer of submarine Shark before World War II, p. 26.

Chi Chi Jima
    Island in Bonin Group which Coye found to have interesting inhabitants in early 1960s, pp. 159-160.

Coye, Beth F., Commander, USN(Ret.)
    Coye's daughter who wrote about status of women in the Navy in the 1970s, pp. 197-199.

Coye, Elizabeth Gabriel
    Meets Coye in childhood, p. 1; has to delay marriage to Coye following his Naval Academy graduation, p. 11; returns to United States from Panama when having baby in 1941, p. 43.

Coye, John S., Jr., Rear Admiral, USN(Ret.) (USNA, 1933)
    Boyhood, pp. 1-6; early memories of Naval Academy, p. 8; graduation from in 1933, p. 9; service in heavy cruiser Northampton in mid-1930s, pp. 12-13; duty as assistant engineer in new destroyer Monaghan in 1930s, pp. 14-23; trained at submarine school in New London in 1937, pp. 23-24; serves as engineer officer in submarine Shark from 1937 to 1941, pp. 24-38; received dolphins and qualifies for command while in the Shark, pp. 28-30; Shark collides with carrier Yorktown in 1940, Coye commended, pp. 30-34; service as executive officer and commanding officer of submarine R-18 in 1941-1942, pp. 39-50; bombed by U.S. Navy plane en route to Bermuda, pp. 45-48; gets letter of commendation for work in proving erroneous route through Panama minefields, pp. 48-50; attends submarine PCO school in spring of 1943, pp. 50-53; ordered to Commander Submarines South Pacific Force in June 1943, pp. 53-57; takes command of submarine Silversides, p. 57; considers submarines for scouting line duty to be poor use of assets, pp. 67-69; describes mental attitude of crew during patrol, pp. 72-73; sinks four Japanese ships during second patrol in Silversides, pp. 75-78; salvages innovative Japanese gun from transport, p. 77; leaves on third patrol in Silversides in December 1943, p. 78; hits several

ships in convoy, pp. 81-82; hits two ships during fourth patrol
in early 1944, pp. 87-92; regrets decision not to fire on Japanese
cruisers off Palau, pp. 88-90; gets 12 hits during fifth patrol
in submarine, pp. 92-100; sinks three Japanese ships on 10 May 1944,
pp. 94-95; sinks converted gunboat off Guam, evades depth charges
for five hours, pp. 97-98; sinks two ships simultaneously,
pp. 98-99; becomes wolf pack commander in September 1944,
pp. 106-112; service in wolf pack under Burt Klakring, pp. 112-116;
ends tour in Silversides, pp. 117-118; serves as instructor at
PCO school in New London in early 1945, pp. 118-123; as operations
officer on staff of Commander Submarine Squadron One at Pearl
Harbor and sets up PCO school there, 1947-1948, pp. 123-125;
as Commander Submarine Division 52 in 1948-1949, p. 125; attends
Armed Forces Staff College, pp. 126-127; as ASW officer on staff of
Operational Development Force, pp. 127-131; commanding officer of
submarine tender Fulton, pp. 131-135; commands Submarine Squadron
Eight, pp. 135-137; attends Naval War College in 1954-1955, pp. 137-140,
serves on staff of Commander Second Fleet, including preparation for
NATO exercise Strike Back, pp. 141-148; commands heavy cruiser
Rochester, the Seventh Fleet flagship, 1958-1959, pp. 149-152;
serves in Strike Warfare Division on OpNav staff, pp. 153-157;
promoted to flag rank and serves as Commander Naval Forces Marianas
from 1961 to 1963, pp. 158-172; commands Amphibious Group Three,
pp. 172-176; serves as deputy chief of staff to CinCSouth, 1964-1966,
pp. 176-183; as Commander Training Command Atlantic Fleet until
retirement in 1968, pp. 184-191; post-Navy life, pp. 192-203.

Earhart, Amelia
    Aviatrix lost in 1930s; remains searched for on Saipan in early
    1960s, pp. 169-170.

Fife, James, Jr., Rear Admiral, USN (USNA, 1918)
    Commander Task Force 72 in South Pacific in World War II, pp. 54-55,
    assigned patrols to submarines on basis of ultra, pp. 65-67.

Firefighting
    Search for remedies after aircraft carrier fires in late 1960s,
    pp. 185-186.

Fulton, USS (AS-11)
    Submarine tender commanded by Coye in 1952-1953, pp. 132-136.

Goding, M. Wilfred
    Capable high commissioner of Pacific Trust Territories in early
    1960s, p. 171.

Guam
    Effects of typhoon Karen in 1962, pp. 161-163; Japanese history
    of, pp. 164-165; Admiral Chester Nimitz's interest in, pp. 168-169;
    current situation of, pp. 170-171.

Harlfinger, Frederick J. II, Lieutenant Commander, USN (USNA, 1935)
    While commanding USS *Trigger* in World War II stages race against USS *Silversides*, pp. 103-104.

Klakring, Thomas Burton, Commander, USN (USNA, 1927)
    Head of submarine wolf pack called "Burt's Brooms" during 1944, pp. 113-114.

Leigh, Charles F., Lieutenant, USN (USNA, 1939)
    Did extremely fine job as executive officer of submarine *Silversides* during World War II, p. 93.

Marianas Islands
    Coye serves as naval commander in the area in the early 1960s, pp. 158-172.

Miquelon Islands
    Destroyer *Monaghan* visits in 1935, pp. 16-17.

Monaghan, USS (DD-354)
    Destroyer in which Coye served from time of commissioning in 1935 through early shakedown cruises and fishing trip for President Franklin D. Roosevelt, pp. 14-23.

NATO
    Description of planning for exercise Strike Back in North Atlantic in 1956, pp. 141-148; Coye's duty on CinCSouth staff in mid-1960s, pp. 176-183.

Naval Academy, U.S.
    Difficulty getting appointment during Depression years, p. 5; only half of class of 1933 commissioned at time of graduation, pp. 9-11.

Naval War College
    Description of in mid-1950s, pp. 137-140.

Navy Tactical Data System (NTDS)
    Development of in 1960s, pp. 187-191.

New Jersey, USS (BB-62)
    Served well as Second Fleet flagship in mid-1950s, pp. 141-142.

Nimitz, Chester W., Fleet Admiral, USN (USNA, 1905)
    Continuing interest in Guam during the 1960s, pp. 168-169.

Northampton, USS (CA-26)
    Heavy cruiser which made voyage to East Coast with U.S. Fleet in 1934, pp. 12-14.

Operational Development Force
    Antisubmarine warfare projects under development around 1950, pp. 127-131.

Palau
   Pacific island which submarine <u>Silversides</u> operated near
   during World War II, pp. 79-82.

Panama
   Patrols by submarines in Panama area at beginning of World War
   II, pp. 41-50.

Pearl Harbor
   Post-World War II submarine operations in the area, pp. 124-125.

Pirie, Robert B., Vice Admiral, USN (USNA, 1926)
   Dashing leader as Commander Second Fleet in 1950s, p. 143.

Prospective Commanding Officers School
   Provides training for submarine skippers during World War II,
   pp. 50-53, 118-123.

<u>R-18</u>, USS (SS-95)
   Coye's service in her in 1941-1942, pp. 39-50; use on patrols of
   Atlantic Coast during World War II, p. 44; bombed by U.S. Navy
   plane en route to Bermuda, pp. 45-48; goes through minefields off
   Panama, pp. 48-50.

<u>Rochester</u>, USS (CA-124)
   Coye commands her in 1958-1959 during her service as Seventh
   Fleet flagship, pp. 149-152.

Roosevelt, President Franklin D.
   Rides destroyer <u>Monaghan</u> for Caribbean fishing trip in
   1930s, pp. 20-22.

Russell, James S., Admiral, USN (USNA, 1926)
   As CinCSouth in 1960s, p. 176; conducts study on aircraft carrier
   fires following retirement, p. 186.

Safety Problems, Naval
   Electric torpedo failure causes explosion under submarine
   <u>Silversides</u> in World War II, pp. 109-110; development of
   new fire fighting agents in wake of carrier fires in 1960s,
   pp. 185-186.

<u>Salmon</u>, USS (SS-182)
   Member of world pack known as "Coye's Coyotes" in 1944, pp. 103-106;
   engaged in surface gun battle with Japanese in October 1944,
   pp. 110-112; joins "Burt's Brooms" wolf pack in late 1944, pp. 112-116.

Second Fleet, U.S.
   Coye's service on fleet staff in mid-1950s during preparations for
   NATO exercise Strike Back, pp. 141-149.

Shark, USS (SS-174)
>Coye's service on board from 1937 to 1941, pp. 24-39; many machinery problems in the boat, pp. 25-27; is run over by the carrier Yorktown in September 1940, pp. 30-34; involvement in fleet war games, pp. 34-35.

Silversides, USS (SS-236)
>Premature explosion of torpedoes causes low morale on Coye's first patrol, pp. 59-64; sinks four Japanese ships on second patrol, pp. 75-78; makes several hits on Coye's third patrol, pp. 78-83; fire breaks out while escaping Japanese submarine, pp. 83-85; sinks three ships on 10 May 1944 while on Coye's fifth patrol, pp. 94-95; sinks converted gunboat off Guam, evades 61 depth charges, pp. 97-98; sinks two ships simultaneously, pp. 98-99; receives overhaul at Mare Island in summer of 1944, pp. 100-102; part of wolf pack on Coye's sixth patrol in September 1944, pp. 106-116; torpedo failure occurs during pursuit of Japanese tanker after Battle of Leyte Gulf, pp. 109-112; reorganized into "Burt's Brooms" wolf pack in November 1944, pp. 112-116; receives Presidential Unit Citation, p. 118; patrol reports on file at Groton, Connecticut, pp. 86-87, 202-203.

Submarines
>Engineering performance in World War II resulted from design deficiencies pointed out before the war, pp. 26-27; R-boats given to Britain, p. 42; remaining R-boats used for patrols during war, pp. 44-45; problems with torpedo exploders during war, pp. 59-63; poor use of submarine scouting lines in the Pacific, pp. 67-69; capabilities of submarines, pp. 69-70; submarine crew rotation system, pp. 70-71; torpedoes improved by 1943, p. 82; wolf packs become prevalent, pp. 104-106; electric torpedo failure causes explosion under the Silversides, pp. 109-110; British X-craft miniature submarines, pp. 128-129.

Torpedoes
>Training with at PCO school in World War II, p. 52; magnetic exploder ineffective when fired from Silversides, pp. 59-63; electric torpedo blows up underneath Silversides, p. 109.

Training
>See: Prospective Commanding Officers School. Coye commands training command for Atlantic Fleet in mid-1950s, pp. 184-190.

Trigger, USS (SS-237)
>Race against sister ship Silversides, pp. 103-104; member of wolf pack under Coye, p. 108; becomes member of "Burt's Brooms" wolf pack in November 1944, pp. 112-116.

Typhoons
>See: Guam.

Vernou, Walter N., Captain, USN (USNA, 1901)
    Amazing memory enabled him to know name of every crew member while commanding heavy cruiser Northampton in 1930s, pp. 36-38.

Vietnam
    Suspicion of sabotage on planes carrying technicians bound for Vietnam in early 1960s, pp. 165-167.

Watlington, Sarah J., Ensign, USN
    Capable woman officer serving on staff in Naples in 1960s, p. 199.

Wellborn, Charles, Jr., Vice Admiral, USN (USNA, 1921)
    Very capable flag officer in command of U.S. Second Fleet in mid-1950s, p. 143.

Wolf packs
    "Coye's Coyotes," pp. 106-112; "Burt's Brooms," pp. 112-116.

Women in the Navy
    Commander Beth Coye's opinions on unfair treatment, pp. 197-199; Admiral Coye's opinion on, pp. 199-202.

Worthington, Robert K., Lieutenant, USN (USNA, 1938)
    Executive officer of submarine Silversides during World War II action in Pacific, pp. 58-59, 92-93.

www.ingramcontent.com/pod-product-compliance
Lightning Source LLC
Chambersburg PA
CBHW080613170426
43209CB00007B/1422

Preface

This volume contains the transcript of several interviews with Rear Admiral Edwin T. Layton, U.S.N. (retired). They were obtained in May, 1970 by Comdr. Etta Belle Kitchen, U.S.N. (retired) at the home of Admiral Layton in Carmel, California and were for the Oral History program of the U.S. Naval Institute in Annapolis, Maryland.

Admiral Layton revised very considerably the transcript of the interviews. The text we have here is in some sense a condensation and a distillation of what he said originally on the tapes. It bespeaks therefore due reflection and consideration for the demands of the historical record and should be valued as such. Layton was in a unique position during World War II to know with great accuracy much of the background to many of the naval events of the Pacific war.

A subject index has been included to facilitate the use of the memoir.

John T. Mason, Jr.,
Director of Oral History
U.S. Naval Institute
Annapolis, Maryland

REMINISCENCES

OF

REAR ADMIRAL EDWIN T. LAYTON

U. S. Navy (Retired)

U. S. NAVAL INSTITUTE

ANNAPOLIS, MARYLAND

1975